Living Without Cruelty

Living Without Cruelty

MARK GOLD

GREEN
PRINT

Green Print
Marshall Pickering
3 Beggarwood Lane, Basingstoke, Hants RG23 7LP, UK

Copyright © 1988 Mark Gold
Recipes: Copyright © 1988 Sarah Brown
First published in 1988 by Green Print
Part of the Marshall Pickering Holdings Group
A subsidiary of the Zondervan Corporation

ISBN 1 85425 000 0

The text is printed on *Five Seasons 100 per cent recycled book paper* made by William Sommerville and Son plc in Scotland.

Phototypeset in 11/12pt Linotron Sabon by
Input Typesetting Ltd, London SW19 8DR.
Printed in Great Britain by
Anchor Brendon Ltd, Colchester, Essex.

Vegetarianism is the diet of the future, as flesh-food is the diet of the past. In that striking and common contrast, a fruit shop side by side with a butcher's, we have a most significant object lesson. There, on the one hand, are the barbarities of a savage custom—the headless carcasses, stiffened into a ghastly semblance of life, the joints and steaks and gobbets with their sickening odour, the harsh grating of the bone-saw, and the dull thud of the chopper—a perpetual crying protest against the horrors of flesh-eating. And as if this were not witness sufficient, here close alongside is a wealth of golden fruit, a sight to make a poet happy, the only food that is entirely congenial to the physical structure and the natural instincts of mankind, that can entirely satisfy the highest human aspirations. Can we doubt, as we gaze at this contrast, that whatever intermediate steps may need to be gradually taken, whatever difficulties to be overcome, the path of progression from the barbarities to the humanities of diet lies clear and unmistakable before us?

Henry Salt 1851–1939
The Humanities of Diet

Acknowledgements

I would like to thank: Emily McIvor for her faith and encouragement, Barry Kew and Adrian Sandeman for reading the manuscript and for offering valuable advice; Amanda Rofe for what must have been many monotonous hours of typing; Sarah Brown for both her generosity and her expertise in supplying the delicious recipes, Gill Langley, Kathryn Reynolds, Robert Sharpe and probably many others, who will spot their influence here or there; and the staff, supporters and Council of Animal Aid, who have helped to make the task of running the Society such a pleasure and a privilege despite the horrors we confront daily.

Contents

LIVING WITHOUT CRUELTY CAMPAIGN

The ideas presented in this book are developed from the Living Without Cruelty Campaign, launched by Animal Aid in 1985. The object has been to spread as widely as possible the message that all those who are sick of stories and pictures of animal abuse can find alternatives. Animal Aid aims to provide the information necessary for each individual to begin the struggle against cruelty to animals, as well as campaigning actively against animal experiments, factory farming and other areas of animal cruelty. In 1987, Animal Aid organized the first Living Without Cruelty Exhibition at Kensington Town Hall, London, with the ideas expressed here demonstrated in one vast celebration of cruelty-free living. For more details of the work of Animal Aid, the Living Without Cruelty Campaign and future exhibitions, contact:

Animal Aid, 7 Castle Street, Tonbridge, Kent, TN9 1BH.

Introduction

Although the main theme of this book is vegetarianism, I will have failed miserably if 'living without cruelty' is interpreted as simply the message of an 'animal lover' or 'health-food addict' praising the niceties of a diet free from animal produce. Admittedly, I have devoted considerable space to the more obviously attractive aspects of vegetarianism, such as the latest information on how your health is likely to benefit, several delicious new recipes from Great Britain's best known vegetarian cook and a guide to the many mouth-watering products now finding their way into the shops. Nor would I wish to undervalue this information, as it proves that the change to an animal-free diet should be seen as an introduction to more healthy and interesting foods, rather than any sort of self-sacrifice. Yet I hope it sounds neither too pious nor pretentious to say that this book is written to appeal more to the human spirit than to our taste-buds.

Living Without Cruelty is aimed at the increasing numbers of people who have become heartily sick of stories and pictures detailing abuse of animals, humans and the environment. It invites everyone both to share and to encourage a life-style which rejects cruelty and exploitation wherever it is possible to do so. Perhaps the main reason why vegetarianism has such a significant role to play in pursuit of such an ideal is that it represents one emphatic and effective action which each of us is able to take in order to demonstrate our opposition to greed, waste and needless bloodshed. So often we feel helpless when we see life and beauty crushed by violence and ugliness, yet vegetarianism offers a real opportunity to resist at least a portion of the world's squalor and misery. This, I believe, explains why many people claim to feel so much healthier only a few weeks after they stop eating meat. Leaving aside the advantages to physical health, the spiritual benefits derived from knowing that no creature has been brutalized in the production of our food should not be underestimated.

Of course, 'living without cruelty' does not end with vegetarianism. On the contrary, a meat-free diet is only the beginning. For example, later in the book I present details of the cruelty-free alternatives now available to the ways in which animals are abused in the research, production or 'safety' testing of a whole range of commodities we use routinely, including garden and agricultural chemicals, household products, drugs, cosmetics and food additives. Nor does 'living without cruelty' end with animals, for one of the arguments crucial to this work is that our desire to reject animal suffering should not be divorced from concern about human injustices. To buy products which ensure a fair deal for the humans that produce them should be accepted as part of the same impulse which prompts us to denounce goods which cause needless damage either to the environment or to other species.

What I am not trying to suggest, however, is some absolute dogma representing *the* approved life-style. Sometimes there are certain to be conflicts of interest between humans and the rest of the natural world which defy easy solutions, and besides, it is the spirit to which 'living without cruelty' appeals which is even more important than any answers it seeks to provide. By cultivating a questioning attitude and by demonstrating how every individual can use their power as a consumer to influence the world in which we live, the aim is to stimulate us all to go on and on searching for a more compassionate life-style. Self-righteousness and complacency are, in fact, the enemies of the 'living without cruelty' philosophy.

I hope that anybody who reads this book will emerge with most of the information necessary to enable them to live healthily without being dependent upon animal suffering. A few indications of how to avoid products involving the abuse of humans and the environment are also added in Part 3 of the book. The excuse, if one is needed, for putting the emphasis on the misery of animals is not that I consider them any more important than humans, but rather because the misconception still persists that their pain is somehow unimportant in a world where human torment is rampant. If this book is to achieve anything, I would like it at least to prove the wisdom of the beliefs expressed so forcefully by the sadly neglected environmentalist, social reformer and defender of animals, Henry Salt (1851–1939):

> Reformers of all classes must recognise that it is useless to preach peace by itself, or socialism by itself, or anti-vivisection by itself, or vegetarianism by itself, or kindness to animals by itself. The cause of each of all the evils that afflict the world is the same—the general lack of humanity, the lack of the knowledge that all sentient life is akin, and that he who injures a fellow-being is in fact doing injury to himself. The prospects of a happier society are wrapped up in this despised and neglected truth, the very statement of which, will, at the present time (I well know) appear ridiculous to the accepted instructors of the people. . . .
>
> As long as man kills the lower races for food or sport, he will be ready to kill his own race for enmity. It is not this bloodshed, or that bloodshed, that must cease, but all needless bloodshed—all wanton infliction of pain or death upon our fellow-beings.[1]

I believe that what the outright rejection of unnecessary bloodshed at the core of vegetarianism represents is crucial to the quest for a less violent and more rational future.

And should all this sound a little too stern and serious, it is a fortunate bonus that a meat-free diet has the added advantage of being as healthy and enjoyable as it is enriching. Just try some of the introductory recipes by Sarah Brown and you will see what I mean.

Mark Gold
Speldhurst, Kent

Part One

CHAPTER ONE

Animal Suffering

Over the past few years a great deal of publicity has been given to the conditions endured by animals in factory farms. To protest about the imprisonment of living creatures in tiny crates and cages, however, is only to scratch the surface of an immense problem. The more we look into the treatment of farm animals the more we find suffering on a massive scale. Without resorting to an examination of every minute detail, this chapter will try to give some indication of the ways in which animals are abused so that we can eat them and suggest that the weight of evidence demands a change in our eating habits. For it is this evidence that must be at the centre of any campaign to promote vegetarianism.

Almost every punishment or violent act we condemn in human society, we sanction in our treatment of farm animals. From birth to death animals are subjected to the types of abuses which, were they inflicted upon humans, would be deplored almost universally.

BREEDING STOCK

Degradation begins with conception. Natural mating in free or even relatively free circumstances is becoming increasingly rare. Artificial insemination is responsible for approximately two-thirds of dairy–cow pregnancies in the UK and is also increasingly common on poultry-breeding farms. Although artificial insemination is not yet practised widely with pigs, there are other indignities to await the

3

unfortunate sow. These include what one farmer has accurately described as 'the rape rack', where females are restrained by tethers, thus allowing boars to detect when they are on heat and to serve them.

At a time when ethical problems associated with interference in the human embryo has become an important and controversial issue, it is revealing that no doubts seem to exist over the application of embryo techniques to farm animals. Indeed it could be argued that farm animals have become the guinea-pigs of scientific developments in this field. Geneticists have discovered that by transferring the embryos of the most productive female cattle into the wombs of less productive animals, it is possible to obtain greater numbers of high-quality calves. This has meant that instead of following their traditional farm roles as calf breeders, some female cattle are now being inseminated repeatedly simply to provide embryos for other animals to carry. By using this method, 'donor' cows can be inseminated up to ten times a year, with the womb 'flushed' each time and the embryo transferred to the receiving 'poorer quality' animals. Pig embryotomy takes a different form. The sow is slaughtered shortly before she is due to farrow and the live piglets are removed soon afterwards. They are then taken to the customer farm in sterile containers. Although pig embryotomy is only practiced in the 'best quality animals' at the moment, it is clearly a practice that may be used more freely in the future.

It is widely recognized that most animals share with humans a highly developed maternal instinct. Anybody who has watched a mother hen strutting proudly around the farmyard with her young or heard the harrowing deep cry of a cow calling in vain for the calf which has recently been taken away from her, will not need further proof of the close bond that exists between mother and young. Perhaps the most moving illustration of this fact is the story which appeared in many national newspapers in December 1983.[1] A heifer named Blackie escaped over a fence in the middle of the night and trekked seven miles through Devon country lanes until she found the eight-week-old calf from whom she had that day been separated at market. Clearly, the level of communication was almost beyond human understanding.

How then does animal farming show respect for this bond? Unweaned calves are taken away from their mothers within the first few days of birth and pigs are forced to give birth in metal farrow crates, the structure of which often show 'an appalling lack of consideration for the needs of the pig'.[2] In crates, pigs are unable to turn around and are confined in a position which allows them only to be convenient milk bars for their young. It is now becoming increasingly common to keep them in crates for up to three weeks until the young are taken away at an unnaturally early age. (Naturally, weaning takes eight weeks.) The logic behind early weaning is that it becomes possible to impregnate the mother again more quickly, thus allowing her to have more pregnancies in her short life. Between five and seven days after the piglets have been taken away, the sow will come back into season and the whole breeding cycle is repeated. The end for breeding cattle and pigs comes literally when the animal is considered clapped out from repeated pregnancies. Lameness, stress and inability to conceive will result quickly in animals being packed off on a lorry bound for the meat-pie factory, probably via the stressful conditions of a market sale. In the wild, both cattle and pigs would live for many years longer.

For poultry there is no association between mother and young at all. Eggs are removed and hatched on farms specially built for the process. Recently, genetic innovation has resulted in the hatching of eggs from specially bred 'dwarf mums'. These are small birds which save money because they eat less food and take up less space but still produce the required strain of chicks for the broiler-chicken industry. The problem created by having 'mini-mums' mating with large males is that 'he is inclined to rape and damage the female'.[3] Consequently, many experts argue that 'the way forward for Britain's broiler industry' is to house the females in cages and to artificially inseminate them.[4]

These examples illustrate the possibilities of life for breeding stock on most farms. First, they are genetically manipulated in order to produce maximum profitability from both them and their progeny. This is followed by giving birth, separation from their young, repeated pregnancies without any chance of expressing maternal instinct and, finally, premature death.

FATTENING STOCK

What happens to the young fattened up for meat, dairy or poultry production? Hundreds of thousands of them fail to live beyond a few days. According to the periodical *Pig Farming*, 'nearly three-quarters of a million healthy piglets starve to death every year'.[5] Furthermore, the constant interference with pig genetics in the search to find a more profitable breed has produced many abnormalities, such as 'a recent spate of piglets born with no anus'.[6] This malformation affects approximately 1% of the national pig herd. (Fifteen million are killed annually). 'Nationally, . . . two million pigs die between birth and weaning'.[7]

Some calves are reared for beef, some go to veal farms, some are exported, while others become dairy cows. The weakest of them are considered uneconomic and, as a result, may be hawked around market auctions before a lucrative price is found. Then they are sold off as 'bobby calves', packed off to the slaughterhouse to provide either meat pies or pet food. Even hardened slaughtermen have said that they find the killing of these pathetic young animals distasteful, particularly when they will suck the human hand in search of comfort. Some calves do not even make it to the slaughterhouse. The President of the British Cattle Veterinary Association has estimated that more than 170 000 die before they are three months old, due largely to 'neglectful husbandry' and 'appalling treatment' at markets.[8] It would be a mistake, however, to think that the mass death of very young farm animals is a problem associated solely with factory farming. Every year between one and three million of those cuddly, newborn lambs die within a few days of birth, mostly from hunger and exposure.[9]

The largest mass slaughter of infant animals involves the factory farming of poultry, specifically the euthanasia of day-old chicks. Poultry geneticists produce two types of birds. One is bred to be fattened for chicken meat and is programmed to put on weight as quickly as possible for the smallest amount of food that can be managed. The other is for the egg industry and is required to lay as many eggs as possible, again keeping down feed costs to a minimum. Roughly 40 million of the latter strain have the misfortune to be born male and, therefore, cannot lay eggs. Because these birds would not put on weight as quickly as the strain fattened for the meat market, they are considered economically useless and consequently they are destroyed at a day old. No laws exist for this mass execution. Birds can be gassed, suffocated or even have their heads crushed against a wooden bar. Their remains form what is called hatchery waste and are mostly sold for fertilizer.

Young animals that survive early slaughter are normally subject to certain mutilations. Piglets have their tails docked and their teeth clipped in order to minimize damage caused by fighting. The fighting itself is largely the result of overcrowding, which may turn normally playful activity into aggression. *Pig Farming* states that 'despite careful clippings the teeth are frequently shattered'.[10] Some hens are debeaked, a painful mutilation which involves cutting through sensitive tissue the equivalent of the quick of a human nail. The main cause of debeaking is once again overconfinement, which tends to stimulate feather pecking and, in extreme cases, cannibalism. Most male pigs are castrated in answer to an old, unproven theory that the meat from undoctored male animals suffers from 'boar taint'. Male calves are also usually castrated. The majority of farm animals are branded and/or have their ears clipped when they are sold at market.

When it comes to actual life on the farm, rearing conditions often consist of life imprisonment, the worst punishment that can be handed out to a criminal under British law. Between 35 and 40 million hens are kept five to a 20 inch-(50 centimetre-) wide cage for egg production, unable to spread their wings, peck in the ground for food, or make a dust bath. Almost 400 000 sows are confined in stalls two feet (60 centimetres) wide, most of them standing throughout their lives on cold and uncomfortable concrete. More than 425 million broiler chicken and 29 million turkeys are fattened up in windowless sheds, over-crowded by the time that they reach slaughter weight. In the search for greater profits, broilers are expected to multiply their weight 50–60 times in their seven weeks of life—a staggering 25 million per year die even before they get to the slaughterhouse because of the strain.[11] Rabbits reared in cages are the latest victim of the factory farm, with more than 2·5 million slaughtered annually in the UK.

Deprivation for all these factory-farm animals is intense. To varying degrees they are denied any possibility of building up a social community, of taking exercise, of feeling the wind or the sun on their backs, of browsing or grooming. Almost everything which makes life worth living for them is excluded.

EXECUTION

Execution follows life imprisonment. The first part of this drawn-out process begins with collection from the farm and transportation to the slaughterhouse. Poultry-transportation lorries are intensely overcrowded with birds stuffed into crates like bits of rag. Sometimes lids or flaps are shut with wings or legs trapped and occasionally birds have their heads caught in the crate above and are hanged. Handling is rough. The Agricultural Department's Advisory Service (ADAS) themselves believe that 'an unacceptable proportion of broilers are damaged during collection and transport; this leads to poor quality carcasses and is also detrimental to the bird's welfare'. They add that 'reliable figures on downgrading losses (i.e. birds with inferior meat quality) are difficult to obtain, but a recent survey of a few large companies indicated a range of 8–25%'.[12] This means that between approximately 30 million and 100 million birds are downgraded, a large proportion being 'due to physical damage, mainly bruising . . . 90% of which occurs within the period of 12 hours before killing'.[12] With larger animals the situation is much the same. Over 50 000 carcases are condemned every year in the UK owing to severe bruising.[13] These are only the extreme examples: one survey of pig carcasses showed over 50% damaged.[14]

When the time comes for slaughter the myth still persists that farm animals are slaughtered humanely, almost in the way that sick dogs are put to sleep. This is a long way from the disturbing truth. Death in modern slaughterhouses is painful, frightening and undignified. In 1984 the UK Government's own advisory committee on matters of farm animal welfare (FAWC), published the *Report on the Welfare of Livestock (Red Meat Animals) at the Time of Slaughter*. It is a remarkably damning document. So much so that had it been published by an animal rights group it would almost certainly have been dismissed as extreme. Despite giving the 40 abattoirs visited ample warning of their impending arrival and purpose, FAWC still found animal abuse wherever they looked. We can only speculate upon what horrors they might have discovered had the slaughterhouse staff not been on their best behaviour.

In their general comments at the beginning of their Report, FAWC stressed that animal welfare has 'low priority' in abattoirs and that existing legislation contained in the Slaughterhouse Act (1974) is often simply ignored.

They attribute negligence to two factors: (a) no member of staff is given overall accountability of welfare; and (b) local authorities are 'not taking their responsibilities seriously enough'. FAWC continued by criticizing the design of slaughterhouses and gave examples of slippery floors, insufficient ventilation and inadequate drinking facilities, contributing to an overall view that 'all too often investment in slaughterhouse improvements has been geared solely to increasing throughput and profitability';

The first specific mention of brutality comes in a brief section on unloading. We are told that 'it was clear that in the hands of some slaughterhouse staff use of the electric goads becomes an automatic act in the process of their handling of all animals, regardless of whether or not the animals were refusing to move forward'. FAWC added that 'we have seen too many cases of random application of the electric goads to the anal or genital areas of the animal'. When animals first arrive at the slaughterhouse they are herded into a resting area, known as the lairage. At this stage, FAWC noted 'some overcrowding', 'no evidence of bedding being available to cover the eventuality of an overnight stay' (contrary to existing legislation) and also problems with animals remaining unfed for long periods prior to slaughter. The next difficulty to be discussed in the *Report* is in moving animals 'fearful of the situation generally in the slaughterhouse—of the noise, smell, handling and strangeness of the surroundings'— from lairage to the stunning area. Once again this is a point where brutality with goads is frequently encountered.

On stunning itself (i.e. rendering animals unconscious before their throats are cut), FAWC 'have concluded that unconsciousness and insensibility are being assumed to exist in many slaughtering operations when it is highly probable that the degree is insufficient to render the animal insensitive to pain'. This was particularly true in the case of pigs, sheep and some calves, all of which are usually stunned by the use of low-level electricity, normally administred by tongs. Breaches of the recommendation for the length of time the tongs should be applied (seven seconds minimum), the minimum voltage (75 volts) and of the correct positioning of the electrodes were common and 'woeful ignorance' of the requirements was found among slaughterhouse staff. FAWC suggest that 'it was all too common for the tongs to be used as a method of catching and immobilising the animal rather than an accurately placed stunning instrument.' As a result, many animals were probably fully conscious when shackled by the back leg and hoisted on the slaughterline to have their throats cut. In the words of Dr Gerlis, a Consultant Pathologist from Leeds, 'electric stunning as carried out in this country at present is clearly a farce. The vast majority of the animals on which this barbaric practice is inflicted are probably just paralysed, but remain fully conscious of the electric shock in addition to the subsequent shackling, hoisting and sticking'.[15]

An article in the periodical *Meat Industry* by 'an authority on all aspects of slaughtering' suggests that defective stunning equipment is also a common fault, turning the death of some farm animals into a 'noisy and doubtless painful nightmare'. It is clear that the captive bolt pistol (the instrument used to stun adult cattle) and the electric tongs are frequently badly maintained, 'treated almost with contempt, being knocked and dropped and in many cases only cleaned when they fail entirely to operate'. The meat industry's 'authority' concludes that 'all the conditions which cause maximum electrical hazards: water, high humidity, corrosive substances (e.g. blood and salt) are present in abattoirs and these combined with indifference and rough usage quickly lead to indifferent stunning results'.[16]

It is generally acknowledged that the most 'humane' method of stunning is the captive bolt pistol, used mostly to shoot adult cattle. Yet according to Dr Gerlis 'it is a horrifying fact that approximately one-third of the cattle shot in this way are not stunned but stand greviously wounded and fully conscious while the pistol is reloaded'.[15] Even when the shot is more accurate, slaughtermen acknowledge the difficulty of deciding when an animal is properly stunned. In the same article one worker says that 'we don't seem able to resolve whether an animal is conscious or semi-conscious, whether you should poke it in the eye when it has been shot once, or whether you should poke it in its eye before it's been shot'.

Poultry fare no better than red-meat animals. In its 1982 *Report on the Welfare of Poultry at the Time of Slaughter*, FAWC produced a similarly appalling picture of animal abuse. Apart from rough handling and other problems of transportation discussed previously, they noted that many birds (moving towards their deaths hung upside down on a moving conveyor belt) were inefficiently stunned, so that 'a substantial number may still be sensitive' when slaughtered. This, combined with faulty slaughtering methods, results in 'some birds entering the scalding tank before they are dead' and others showing 'obvious signs of consciousness'. In their general summary FAWC stated that they had 'much sympathy' with 'the view that the nature of the slaughterhouse operation, the high degree of mechanisation and their speed and scale, results in sentient creatures being treated with indifference'.

These are the conditions which greet some eight million chickens, 300 000 pigs, 80 000 cattle, more than 500 000 turkeys, 50 000 rabbits and 300 000 sheep every week. Rather than deluding ourselves with some myth about 'humane' killing conditions, is it not time that the sheer volume of blood, the nauseating smell as the steam rises from the warm flesh of executed creatures, the deafening noise and the cold mechanized death which awaits more than one million animals every day in the UK alone should draw us to question 'the sickness of spirit that has made us willing accomplices in the Auschwitz-like mass slaughter'?[17]

Of course, it is as much a myth to suppose that in some distant past era slaughter was more gentle. Graphic accounts of the death of family-reared cottage pigs in nineteenth-century Britain demonstrates that the killing was never pleasant. In Thomas Hardy's *Jude the Obscure*, we read:

> Arabella opened the sty door. Together they hoisted the victim onto the stall, legs upwards and while Jude held him Arabella bound him down, looping the cord over his legs to keep him from struggling. . . .
> The animal's note changed its quality. It was not now rage, but the cry of despair; long drawn, slow and hopeless. The blood flowed out in a torrent instead of the trickling stream she had desired. The dying animal's cry assumed its third and final tone, the shriek of agony; his glazed eyes riveting themselves on Arabella with the eloquently keen reproach of a creature recognising at last the treachery of those who had seemed his only friends.[18]

Again, in Flora Thompson's two semi-autobiographies about rural Oxfordshire, *Larkrise* and *Over to Candleford*, we have two detailed accounts of slaughter. In the first we are told that 'the killing was always a noisy, bloody business, in the course of which the animal was hoisted to a rough bench that it might bleed through. The job was often bungled, the pig often getting away and having to be chased.'[19] In the second description, five-year-old Laura looks on at the newly killed pig, 'patting its hard, cold side and wondering that a thing so alive and full of noise could be so still'.[19]

As ghastly as the whole business clearly was, in some ways we have travelled a long way backwards from those primitive scenes of bloodshed. At least killing animals was once considered necessary for food and people took responsibility for raising animals themselves and also for the killing. As Flora Thompson demonstrates in the following quotation, slaughtering an animal, which 'had

13

lived' with the family was a matter of emotional significance to everybody involved and nobody treated it lightly:

> She had known that pig all its life. Her father had often held her over the door of its sty to scratch its back and she had pushed lettuce and cabbage stalks through the door for it to enjoy. Only that morning it rooted and grunted and squealed because it had had no breakfast. Her mother had said its noise got on her nerves and her father looked uncomfortable . . .[19]

Nowadays, slaughter is not only bloody and barbaric but also a highly mechanized business, where literally thousands of animals can pass along a conveyor-belt system every hour in the killing factory. Even leaving aside the greater number of animals killed nowadays, we have also to ask whether we have progressed in our attitudes merely by hiding the grisly business out of our sight. Everything has been neatly arranged to ensure that meat is now simply food on our plates. Not for us any emotional significance in its production. Others do our dirty work in the abattoir and we are left with only the reassuring advertisements, comforting us with a variety of soothing images. Sometimes we even see cartoon presentations of animals merrily giving their lives for our enjoyment, accompanied by slogans such as 'I want to be your ham'.

Concerned that the public is beginning to question the slaughter of animals for food, our modern meat trade intends to go even further in its attempt to 'conjure up an image of meat devoid from the animal or the act of slaughter itself'.[20] They argue that most of the public do not want to be made aware of the bloodier side of the meat trade and that they should put their efforts into dispelling any association whatsoever between meat and animals. Suggestions include: changing workers in the meat trade into red overalls to avoid 'adverse reactions' created by blood-spattered white coats; changing the name of abattoirs and slaughterhouses to meat plants or meat factories: and changing the name butchers to victuallers. Already, poultry slaughterhouses have become known as 'poultry processing plants'.

No effort is being spared to protect us from considering the misery which produces our pound of flesh and most of us are only too glad to be part of the deception. Ultimately, however, no ingenious slogans can destroy the stench of death or clean the abattoir floors treacherous with blood and guts. Nor can they hide the misery of the rearing conditions on factory farms, deaden the anguished squeals or hide the dying struggles of the 500 million animals which are killed annually in British 'plants' alone. All of this for the type of food we do not need.

OVER-EMOTIVE?

To some people the words I have chosen to explain life for farm animals will be dismissed as over-emotive. 'Life imprisonment', 'solitary confinement', 'euthanasia of young', 'anguished squeals', 'execution', etc: these are descriptions usually applied to human existence, not to the fate of other species. Indeed, in many ways our exploitation of other animals is based on the justification that they are incapable of experiencing joy or sorrow or any other emotion comparable to humans. Yet to accept such a theory nowadays is to ignore both the indisputable logic of the case for radical changes in our attitude to other animals and the moral dilemma with which our ever increasing knowledge of animal behaviour is confronting us.

The more we learn about animals the more fascinating we find them. Wildlife programmes are among the most popular on television, glossy publications extolling the wonders of nature proliferate on the book market and bird and nature reserves are enthusiastically supported by the general public. If there was ever an excuse for mistreatment of animals and birds on the grounds that they are inferior creatures lacking in intelligence and feeling, then science is continually destroying it. Dedicated studies of how animals behave in their natural habitat have helped to prove conclusively that all living creatures live lives worthy of our respect and wonder, even though their intelligence may often be of a different nature from human responsiveness.

Recent discoveries prove that 'to varying degrees many species have sophisticated forms of communication'. Enlightened psychologists, zoologists, anthropologists and philosophers are all being forced to the view that 'while no animal except the human one has the ability to use a grammatical language capable of handling concepts, there is mounting, indisputable evidence that animals think, assess their options and plan'.[21] One by one, every rationalization put forward over the centuries to excuse our brutalities towards other species is being ridiculed. 'Almost every week', Michael Bright concludes in his book *Animal Language* 'scientific journals report new and ever more astonishing abilities of animals, abilities which we never suspected'.[22] This statement is as valid for farm animals as it is for chimpanzees or squirrels: the fact that it does not suit our traditional concept of farm animals as 'only' creatures reared to satisfy our eating habits should no longer be allowed to exempt us from the realization that they too have the same feelings and intelligence as either creatures in the wild or our domestic pets.

We have already cited the example of the almost incredible level of communication between mother and young cattle, while pigs are known to be every bit as intelligent as cats and dogs. Professor Van Putten, the Dutch ethologist who has made a vast study of pig behaviour, has noted their wide vocabulary and complex behaviour, which includes love of comfort, fun and bathing on hot days and vigorous skin care,[23] *The Biologist* reports that pigs are closer to humans than most other animals and the National Farmers Union has even gone so far as to organize a 'Porkabright Award' for pig intelligence. Among the entries was a sow with 11 piglets who escaped from the rear of her farrowing crate and calmly liberated other sows in the building by nosing up all the backsliding boards, pigs capable of undoing pig-proof bolts and others who distinguish the gear change of a particular Landrover. While this does not constitute conclusive proof of an intelligence similar to humans, it does demonstrate a quality of life which demands far greater respect than the indignities and brutalities handed out on factory farms and in slaughterhouses. Interestingly, were you to imprison a dog throughout its life in the conditions endured by many pigs, you would be liable to prosecution under The Protection of Animals Act (1911).

THE DILEMMA

We are all guilty of irrational contradictions in our attitudes to animals. Why do we decry the eating of horse flesh as an unsavoury foreign habit, yet tuck in to cow flesh unquestioningly? Why do we hang out nuts in our gardens and marvel at the athleticism of wild birds and then feast on poultry? Why does the law make it an offence to keep a canary in a cage where it cannot spread its wings and yet allow the same fate to be inflicted upon poultry?

Given all this, we face a very real dilemma. On the one hand, every necessity or intellectual justification that has ever been put forward for using animals in food production is constantly undermined by what we learn about the capacity for life in all living creatures. On the other, some scientists, employed by commercial companies or motivated by self-glory or obsessive scientific curiosity, are reducing animals to an even lower status than they have ever suffered before, content to inflict upon them whatever abuses commercialism and scientific ingenuity dictate. The choice is a future where animals are free from human prescription or a world created by geneticists who see animals only as a selection of genes to be crossed and mixed mercilessly in the search for greater productivity. Already in this country we have seen the production of the chimera (half-goat, half-sheep) and the suggestion of a woolly pig to produce both wool and cheaper meat. Scientists believe ultimately that by transferring genetic traits between unrelated species they can produce both 'super animals' and dramatically increase the speed of maturation, height and weight.

This view sees animals as nothing more than a complex collection of chemicals. Indeed, the more extreme geneticists are already presenting themselves as the heroes who 'have the technology to rescue the meat industry from its many problems', with research underway to produce a 'super race of cattle, sheep and pigs which will grow bigger, leaner and faster'. In the words of agricultural biochemist Professor David Armstrong, 'I see nothing wrong with the creation of a new species of animal that is more suitable for human consumption than those we have eaten in the past'.[24] In June 1987, Britain's first commercial company offering genetic services to agricultural research and industry was set up. Among the aims of Animal Biotechnology Ltd of Cambridge are to 'convert cows into chemical factories that can be milked for drugs' and to 'enable a dairy cow to give birth to an Aberdeen Angus, or allow the transplant of an embryo from one species into a second which becomes a surrogate mother'.[25]

It is against this reductionist philosophy that vegetarian reverence for all life is needed more urgently than ever before. In a world full of irreverence and contradictions in its treatment of the natural world, it is still possible to assume a life-style which reduces the suffering of other creatures to an absolute minimum. We do not need to kill animals for food, with all the inevitable misery involved, and, whatever scientists tell us to the contrary, there is no such thing as 'a new species of animal that is more suitable for human consumption'. In which case, are we not left with vegetarianism as the only logical response to our growing awareness of animal intelligence and integrity?

CHAPTER TWO

Human Health

Although modern medical orthodoxy has proved remarkably reluctant to recognize the correlation, it is now
becoming widely accepted that what we eat has a
profound effect upon our health. Diet reform is seen as an
important weapon in the battle against death and disease.

For our present purposes, the question is not only the
total significance of food upon our well-being, but, more
specifically, whether or not vegetarianism is healthier than
a diet based upon animal products. As we shall see, there
is now mounting evidence to indicate that in many ways
it is. Before revealing precisely why, it is prudent to suggest
a few qualifications. First, there are enormous differences
between 'good' and 'bad' vegetarian diets. (What exactly
constitutes a good diet will be discussed later.) Second,
while a properly balanced vegetarian diet is generally
speaking good for health, it would be ludicrous to suppose
that switching to vegetarianism on health grounds is an
automatic ticket to active old age. We have all known
individuals who have eaten healthily throughout their lives
and yet have suffered constantly from illness. Alternatively, there are people who live totally on junk food diets
of, for example, sausages, chips and cream cakes and yet
survive to a ripe old age in the best of physical shape. Diet
is only one vital part of a whole range of influences. Work
and home conditions, air, water and chemical pollution,
food additives, tobacco, alcohol and emotional stress are
among other factors which can be grouped broadly as
environmental influences. While these are all to some

extent within our own influence, it is, alas, largely imposs-ible to alter other factors, particularly hereditary genetic causes of disease. In addition, we must accept that as we are all individuals with our own peculiar anatomies, there can never be one precise diet perfectly suited to the needs of the whole human race. All that can be offered here is a summary of mounting evidence which indicates reduced incidence of some of the most prevalent diseases in Western civilization among vegetarians. This is impressive enough without making any exaggerated claims.

OFFICIAL REPORTS ON HEART DISEASE

The last five years have seen numerous publications extol-ling the virtues of this or that food, vitamin or mineral and condemning others. Because of the difference in emphasis among these, there has been a tendency for the food industry to argue that there is neither sufficient evidence nor a concensus of opinion upon which to implement any firm decisions about which foods are either beneficial or harmful. However, yet more remarkable than the differ-ences between the dietary recommendations are the simi-larities. Hardly any disinterested nutritionist argues against radical reductions in sugar, salt and, what most concerns us here, fat, particularly animal fat. Conversely, all experts recommend a significant increase in the consumption of fibre. Recommendations may vary as to the degree by which we should increase or decrease consumption, but almost all informed opinion agrees upon the types of food which are either good or bad for us.

The most serious illness in the UK is heart disease, responsible for the death of 180 000 people every year. A link between this epidemic and diet is now indisputable. In recent years it has provoked reports by two different Government-sponsored committees. In 1984 the Committee on Medical Aspects of Food Policy (COMA) made recommendations 'mainly concerned with dietary changes to decrease the incidence of coronary heart disease' in the UK. They suggested reductions in the amounts of saturated fats we eat and 'compensating for reduced fat intake with increased fibre-rich carbohydrates'. The COMA report added that 'animal protein is often associated with fat that is rich in saturated fatty acids whereas vegetable protein may be associated with dietary fibre'.[1]

The other relevant Government-sponsored report has been surrounded by controversy. In 1979, the National Advisory Committee on Nutrition Education (NACNE) set up a working party to investigate the British diet, under the professorship of Dr James, a well-respected nutritionist. Unfortunately, because of the presence of representatives of both Government and the food industry on NACNE (who worked hand-in-glove to oppose radical change) stringent efforts were made to block Dr James' completed report, which stated unequivocally that our highly processed fat, sugar- and salt-laden diet is a significant factor in the main diseases of Western civilisation. As a result of manoeuvering by vested interests the report failed to appear for almost three years after its completion. After constant lobbying, what has since become known as the NACNE Report did finally emerge, published only as 'a discussion paper'. Practically no publicity was given to its release and it is evident that the Government, influenced by the food industry, was anxious to play down its significance. At this point Geoffrey Canon, then a journalist from *The Sunday Times*, and Caroline Walker, a nutritionist who had been associated with NACNE, 'rescued' the report and translated the recommendations into 'everyday language'. This translation became the basis of their best-selling book *The Food Scandal*.

The NACNE Report states that meat and dairy products (both high in saturated fats) make up about 60% of our total consumption of fat and should be reduced 'very substantially'. 'Instead', we are told, 'We should eat more cereal products, beans and other vegetables—sources of polyunsaturated fats'.[2] Put very simply, the difference between saturated and polyunsaturated fats is as follows. The former are usually solid and tend to make the blood sticky, causing clots and other damage to the arterial walls. Sometimes this eventually leads to heart attacks. Polyunsaturated fats usually occur in liquid form, tend to make the blood smooth and in small quantities are considered beneficial to health. Meat and dairy fats are saturated. Vegetable fats are polyunsaturated. The only exceptions are coconut and palm oils and also some of the blended vegetable oils used in margarine and cheap cooking fats.

All recent reports suggest a reduction in saturated fat intake, though they seem to vary as to what represents a safe level. Recommendations range from a 5–50% reduction. Most estimates are themselves a compromise, recognizing both the practical difficulties of enforcing radical change upon a population conservative in its food habits and also the political problems of disrupting both the current agricultural system and food industry, both based extensively upon animal products and fats. The general message seems to be that the less saturated fat you consume, the less possibility you have of contracting heart problems. (Small quantities of saturated fats are necessary, but these are obtained in sufficient quantities on almost any diet.)

CHOLESTEROL AND HYPERTENSION

Another substance associated with heart problems is cholesterol. This is the name given to a substance which builds up in the arteries and is held responsible for causing blockages in circulation. Reducing cholesterol levels decreases the possibility of death from heart attacks. Cholesterol is only found in animal foods: meat, cream, lard, suet, creamy milk, butter, cheese. Once again the degree to which it should be excluded from our diet is open to debate. Some nutritionists state that any reduction is better than none, while *Farmers Weekly* argues that 'it takes almost a vegetarian diet to make any measurable difference in blood cholesterol levels'.[3] In the eyes of the farming press, such a statement is enough to dismiss the whole subject as wildly impractical. Many healthy vegetarians know otherwise.

Hypertension (i.e. high blood pressure) is another condition thought to predispose sufferers towards heart attacks. In a study published in *The Lancet* in 1983, in which diets were compared, blood pressure fell among patients on a vegetarian diet and went up whenever meat was introduced. Whilst acknowledging the difficulties in drawing firm conclusions, the researchers felt that animal flesh was the food most likely to push up blood pressure.[4] This theory found support in research conducted by Dr Lindahl and associates in Sweden in 1984. A group of 29 patients, all volunteers aged between 25 and 70, had all suffered from high blood pressure for over a year. A strict vegan diet (i.e. no animal produce at all) was introduced and they were all also forbidden chocolate, coffee, tea, sugar and salt. Exercise was encouraged. When the study began all 29 patients were taking drugs which had either failed to lower their blood pressure or had caused unpleasant side-effects. A year later all 26 patients who had persevered with the vegan diet had significantly lower blood pressure, cholesterol levels and pulse rates and all but six of them no longer needed any drug treatment. As *The Times* stated, 'the benefits of the vegan path seem clear'.[5]

CANCER

Cancer is the second biggest killer disease in the UK. It kills 135 000 people every year and debilitates many others. It has been estimated that at least 80% of cancers have environmental causes and are, therefore, theoretically preventable. Diet is one of the principal factors. A report published in the USA in 1977 concluded that it accounts for 40% of cancer among American males, and 65% among females.[6] In the UK an article in *The Lancet* in

1983 suggested that diet is responsible for 35% of all cancers.[7] As with all statistical data, the actual percentages are largely irrelevant; what is important is that medical opinion is more or less united in the belief that diet is almost as crucial a cause of cancer as smoking. More specifically there are growing volumes of clinical research which indicate that a vegetarian diet may reduce the threat from some cancers. It is particularly noticeable that most of the alternative therapies which treat cancer patients through food reform involve either dramatically reducing or cutting out meat completely. As Leon Chaitow states in *An End to Cancer* 'a diet low in animal protein would appear to keep the body immunisation system (its defence mechanism) in a more actively alert state, enabling it to deal effectively with any early cancer developments'.[8]

A study of more than 100 000 people over 16 years by the Epidemiological Department of the National Cancer Research Institute in Tokyo has revealed that 'the absence of daily vegetables in the diet seems to increase the risk of a wide range of cancers'. Participants in this research were divided into 16 groups according to whether or not they consumed cigarettes, alcohol, meat and daily vegetables. The group least susceptible to cancer proved to be those who 'did not smoke, drink or eat meat, but who ate vegetables daily.' Tests also demonstrated that even among those who did smoke, drink or eat meat, there was less cancer risk if vegetables were consumed regularly. Speculating on the results, Dr. Haragna, in charge of the Tokyo research team, believed that 'Beta-Carotene, vitamin C and fibre could be active ingredients in vegetables which reduce cancer risk'.[9] This theory supports to a large extent the advice to all American citizens from the US National Cancer Institute: 'eat more fresh fruit and vegetables'.[10]

Several studies indicate that vegetarian women appear to be less prone to breast cancer than those who eat animal produce. Different oestrogen levels are the vital factor, though there are several alternative viewpoints on exactly how lower levels of the hormone (associated with vegetarian diets) actually reduce the risk of contracting the disease. One study in the USA compared the effects on blood, bowel and urine of vegetarian and non-vegetarian diets and concluded that the larger bowel motion of the former resulted in larger excretions of oestrogen. The researchers felt that the presence in the system of high levels of the hormone may be linked with instances of breast cancer and therefore, strict vegetarianism or veganism reduces the possibility.[11] Another study in the USA and published in the *Journal of the National Cancer Institute* speculated that lower cancer rates among vegetarian females could be explained simply by the fact that they produced less oestrogen in the glands. They offered the same explanation for the lower risk of womb cancer.[12] A third study at Oregon State University linked lower levels of oestrogen in the blood of vegetarian women with a lower likelihood of breast cancer. In this study, the theory was also advanced that avoidance of dairy produce further removes inflation and congestion, thought possibly to be a pre-cancerous state.[13]

Cancer of the colon is the most serious of a host of bowel disorders less likely to occur in vegetarians. By comparing diets in the Western World with those of Third World communities where cancer and other bowel disorders are largely unknown, it has been discovered that the vital food lacking in our diets is fibre. Fibre is only found in vegetarian foods, consequently vegetarians 'consume over twice the national average'. Its main benefit is that it quickens the flow of food through the lower gut and bowel. As fibre processes through the digestive system 'it absorbs liquid and becomes bulky, like a sponge'. This allows the muscles of the intestines to 'get a good grip and move its contents along smoothly, quickly and efficiently'. If there is insufficient fibre taken, then it becomes impossible to absorb water in the digestive tract and consequently waste can become hard and dry and can stick in the intestines. Eventually this waste can putrefy and break down into irritating pockets of fermentation. By contrast, 'the overall effect of high levels of fibre is to prevent straining and to dilute the waste matter in stools which are the potential causes of cancer'.[14]

The need for a high-fibre diet relates to the fact that humans possess the physiology of vegetarian animals rather than carnivores. The latter usually have a short bowels so that the flesh can pass quickly through the system, thus avoiding the above described process of putrefaction. The human intestinal tract is at least four times as long as that of most meat-eating animals, indicating yet again the need for the slow fermentation of food associated with a fibre-rich diet. Reducing meat intake and increasing consumption of fibre reduces the risk of not only cancer of the colon, but also other bowel complaints such as diverticular disease, piles and constipation. All these are common problems in the West. Even moderate reform groups like the Health Education Council have sponsored full page advertisements in national newspapers suggesting that we should eat 'maybe half as much again of fibre at the expense of meat, poultry, eggs, fish, dairy products and sugary things'.[15] They also suggest that such dietary changes would help to overcome another of our common ills—obesity.

Other epidemiological studies seem to confirm the findings of the research we have so far discussed. For instance, the increase in heart disease in Israel between 1960 and 1973 coincided with massive increases in meat consumption and a fall in grain and cereal intake.[16] In New Zealand, where a powerful dairy industry ensures that butter intake per head is the highest in the world and other full-fat dairy produce is consumed to excess, they also have one of the highest coronary disease rates in the world, a national problem with obesity and the highest cancer of the colon rates in the 35 to 64 age group'.[17]

HEALTHY VEGGIES

It is remarkable how similar most of the conclusions reached by the increasing number of studies on the health of vegetarians actually are. A study conducted by John Dickenson of Surrey University and Dr Jill Davis of the South Bank Polytechnic has found that vegetarians suffer less from diet-related illness, spend less time in hospital and save the nation many millions of pounds a year as a result. According to their report, 'meat-eaters had a much higher incidence of constipation, appendicitis, gallstones, angina, haemorrhoids, varicose veins and anaemia and where vegetarians suffer from these diseases it tends to be much later in life'.[18] A comparative study at the University of Oxford has shown that vegetarian women are only half as liable to suffer from gallstones as flesh-eaters:[19] an HMSO booklet *Prevention and Health: Eating for Health* has stated that 'appendicitis is almost unknown in countries where the diet contains less fat, almost no sugar, is rich in cereal foods and therefore contains more dietary fibre'.

The British Medical Association has stated that 'vegetarians have lower rates of obesity, coronary heart disease, high blood pressure, large bowel disorders, and cancers and gallstones.'[20]

T. A. B. Sanders at the Department of Nutrition, Queen Elizabeth College has concluded that 'the few well controlled studies made so far have provided no evidence that vegans and vegetarians are less healthy than omnivores'. Moreover, he found that both vegetarians and vegans were 'lighter in weight' and therefore less likely to suffer from obesity.[21] (Research at the Dunn Nutrition Unit, Cambridge, also noted the 'consistent leanness'[22] of vegetarians.) He added that since obesity 'is well known to be associated with decreased life expectancy and a higher incidence of several diseases such as gout, gallstones, diabetes, mellitus, hypertension and cardiovascular disease ... vegan and vegetarian diets may exert a

27

beneficial effect'. He also reports that the levels of cholesterol, blood pressure, plasma viscosity and clotting factor were found to be lower in vegans than omnivores. His summary reaffirms the view that 'the consumption of a properly balanced vegan and vegetarian diet does not endanger health and the vegan diet in particular may offer important advantages to the health of adults as vegans are less prone to several of the diseases of affluence'.[21]

Researchers at the University of Surrey in 1985 compared the dietary habits of 37 people from four groups: vegans, wholefood vegetarians, wholefood meat-eaters and 'ordinary meat-eaters'. Interestingly, they concluded that 'those people on mere vegan or vegetarian diets can more easily meet currently approved dietary goals as recommended by the National Advisory Committee on Nutritional Education'. The only vitamins in the vegan diet which fail to meet the recommended levels were B12 and Riboflavin (B2). The lacto-vegetarian diet met all the recommended levels, but 'fat levels were too high'. Both the wholefood and the 'ordinary' meat diets showed excess levels of energy obtained from saturated fats, leading to the conclusion that 'there is growing evidence that excess consumption of animal protein can be harmful, leading to calculi formation, raised plasma lipid and blood pressure levels and a higher incidence of carcinogen formation from bile acid'. Researchers recommended restricting consumption of flesh foods to twice a week at most.[23]

By far the most detailed work comparing vegetarian, vegan and flesh diets is currently being undertaken at the University of Oxford. Since it began in 1980, the Oxford long-term study has recruited more than 6000 vegetarians and vegans and just over 5000 meat-eaters from comparable social backgrounds. Volunteers have completed extensive questionnaires, kept four-day 'diet diaries' and given blood samples. While the work is still at a preliminary stage, a pattern is already emerging, confirming most other evidence. Already it seems that the typical vegan diet is closest to the levels of fat, protein and carbohydrates recommended by the NACNE Report. Meat-eaters are consuming more calories, but less fibre than vegetarians and vegans. Vegans have only half the level of cholesterol in their blood compared to meat-eaters, with vegetarians falling in between the two groups. Similarly, vegans have much less LDL cholesterol—the form linked most closely with heart disease.[24]

No evidence promoting vegetarianism on health grounds can be conclusive. Nevertheless, a disinterested study of all the evidence available from clinical trials indicates clearly that a diet free from animal proteins does seem to have potential to minimize the risk of some of the main diseases of affluence with which we are now faced. Finally, a word of warning to those who would attempt to minimize fat intake by switching from red to white meat. Many people have now taken this path, so that while red-meat sales slump and various studies, such as the 1986 report by Euromonitor conclude that 'red meat remains essentially outside the most healthy diet',[25] there is a steady rise in poultry sales. Indeed, the latter is often presented as a health food, when in fact, there are many scientists who believe that there is little difference between red and white meats. In Australia, the National Heart Foundation has officially recommended lean red meat above white meat! In the words of one American doctor, 'What may surprise many people is that dairy products, poultry and seafood also contain a great deal of fat and cholesterol. These foods are not very different from beef and pork in terms of fat and cholesterol, when compared with vegetables which are cholesterol free'.[26]

To summarize in the words of the authors of *The Food Scandal*, 'from a health point of view there is almost everything to be said for vegetarianism. If you don't eat meat, and at the same time take some trouble to eat a wide range of cereals and vegetable products, you are likely to become healthier than meat-eaters'.[27]

CHAPTER THREE

Meat and Drugs

Thus far, we have investigated possible health risks which may be inherent to consumption of large quantities of animal produce. In this chapter we shall move on to consider those hazards created specifically by modern methods of meat production, particularly the use of drugs to increase profitability.

DRUGS

Over the past two decades pharmaceutical companies have begun to derive handsome profits from the livestock industry. In the USA, what has become known as the animal health business is estimated at 2·5 billion dollars.[1] In the UK we enjoy the dubious distinction of being the sixth biggest users of drugs in animal production world-wide.[2]

Drugs have become an indispensable part of modern livestock production. If we look at pig production, for instance, we find that every stage of breeding and fattening involves some sort of pharmaceutical treatment, often to compensate for the unnatural pressure put upon animals in factory farms. Almost as soon as they are born, piglets reared for bacon, pork and ham are subject to their first treatment of antibiotics, as are their mothers, who are fed low levels throughout their continuous cycle of pregnancies. Sows may also be given drugs to induce birth at a convenient time for the stockman. After the pigs have been weaned at an unnaturally early age, usually between

18 and 25 days, and thus deprived of the antibodies supplied by their mother's milk, they are particularly susceptible to disease. Consequently, 'antibacterial' is included in their high protein 'starter ration', both to promote growth and to control swine dystentery. This continues until the pigs have grown sufficiently and are ready to move onto their 'grower ration'. Once again low levels of antibiotics are included. And so it goes on until slaughter. In the words of *Farmers Weekly*, modern methods of pig production often 'involve administering a low level of drugs to stock regularly over a long period or maybe for life'.³ As well as routine doses of drugs added to feed, pigs are susceptible to many diseases, forcing special veterinary medicines to be administered to the whole herd regularly. A whole herd is treated because individual attention is impossible in overcrowded conditions.

Breeding stock fare no better as far as disease and drugs are concerned. Most sows kept confined are prone to a whole host of problems, noticeably respiratory and reproductive diseases. 'In slaughterhouse surveys nearly 50% of pigs show evidence of the typical purple pneumonic lesions on the tip of the lung lobes'.⁴ New infections plague the industry regularly and as soon as one is conquered another rears its head. One recent problem has been named as 'VD in pigs'. According to the journal *Pig Farming* 'it certainly has become a common thing to see a sow discharging heavily'. The cause of this 'kind of epidemic' is unknown. 'Fortunately', the journal adds, 'the condition is . . . pretty responsive to antibiotics'.⁵ Yet another in a long list of complaints viewed simply as a challenge to routine drug therapy.

There is now mounting evidence to suggest that such automatic use of drugs may be responsible for health problems in humans because of what is known as transferable drug resistance. When animals are routinely fed antibiotics, the drugs do not simply destroy harmful bacteria in the gut; beneficial, protective bacteria are also killed.

In turn, the gut may then be invaded by more hardy and dangerous strains, capable of developing resistance to a whole range of antibiotics. Such resistance may then eventually be passed on to humans when they consume meat, milk and eggs. When this pattern emerges it can render antibiotics in human medicine ineffective against an enormous range of infections. Patients may suffer prolonged illness and, in some cases, even death, having been treated with medicines rendered ineffective by transferable resistance. Drugs useful in human treatments, such as ampecillin and penicillin, are heavily prescribed in factory farms.

Although the farming industry insist that there is no proof that drug resistance is passed on from animals to humans in this way, many scientists believe that the evidence is now compelling. The most detailed studies available have been conducted in the USA, particularly by Dr Stewart Levy, Professor of Medicine and Molecular Biology and Microbiology at the Tufts University School of Medicine in Boston. After many years of investigation, Dr Levy is convinced that drug resistance' is 'a highly transferable trait'. His answer to those who dispute his opinion is as follows:

What I would like to ask all those drug companies who claim that antibiotic resistance isn't being spread around farm animals to man is this: Where do you think it is coming from? . . .

What happens for instance when these animals are finally killed? Their offal which is full of micro-organisms, has to be disposed of and their carcasses, which also contain tremendous amounts of bacteria, have to be handled, cut, packaged, shipped, and re-handled. The meat and by-products are moved all over the country, finally coming into contact with the consumer, so I don't see how anyone can say that there is not much possibility of bacterial crossover.[6]

In Great Britain it is true that we do have stricter regulations to control drugs in animal husbandry than in the USA, but it is generally recognized that these regulations have failed to control similar dangers. In the words of the *British Medical Journal*, 'Current regulations on the use of antibiotics in animals bred for food have failed to prevent the rapid emergence of multiple drug resistances'.[7]

Scientists are united in the view that 'the primary source of (salmonella) infection is farm animals',[8] caused by both routine use of antibiotics and the hawking of young calves at market. Many calves are hawked around markets by dealers until a lucrative sale is achieved. This practice of mixing calves creates a huge cocktail of bugs amongst weak and susceptible animals. In 1982, 65 deaths occurred in the UK attributable to salmonellosis. Up until now these have been almost exclusively among high-risk groups, mainly the very old and very young, but with more drugs-resistant strains developing all the time the fear is that 'we might be faced with an epidemic in food animals with the same potential for human illness as typhoid'.[7] *Farmers Weekly* states: 'Britain is sitting on a salmonella time bomb. There are not enough effective drugs to treat it'.[9] To make matters worse it is estimated that only 10 per cent of normal salmonella infections are ever notified to the authorities. There are also other similar infections in humans for which meat is responsible. For example, Dr Wray of the Ministry of Agriculture has stated that 'campylobacterici from meat and milk are responsible for even more gastroenteritis than salmonella'.[10]

HORMONES

Hormone treatment has been applied to cattle for the same profit-making reasons as antibiotics. It also creates similar dangers. Although there is still considerable dispute as to how hormones actually promote weight gain in animals, their effectiveness is beyond doubt.

After pressure from consumer organizations, EEC

ministers felt that by the end of 1985 they could no longer legitimize the application of growth-promoting hormones and voted to ban their use completely. Despite British objections on the grounds that 'it flies in the face of scientific evidence', the UK became the first EEC nation to implement the ban, which officially came into effect in December 1986. (It did, however, continue to fight the ban in the EEC court throughout 1987.)

Whether this action will prove effective is, however, open to considerable doubt. The meat industry admits that 'it will find itself woefully short of arguments to guarantee produce is hormone free' since 'the new laws are full of holes'.[11] There are no adequate procedures for monitoring. Currently, only approximately 300 beef carcasses a year are chosen for random tests out of the 4·2 million animals slaughtered. Whilst new measures will eventually be introduced Ministry of Agriculture officials admit that 'it is extremely difficult to test effectively for hormones'.[12] According to *Meat Trades Journal*, the 'secret fear' of veterinary authorities is 'a switch in the techniques for advertising hormones' in order to defeat any methods of control that might be introduced.

Most disturbing of all, many authorities are convinced that the ban will simply act as an incentive to the black marketing of hormones. In the words of one expert, 'what will happen is a flourishing black market of hormones as happens in parts of Europe'.[11] Some would say that a black market is already thriving far too much for comfort! In 1985, a spate of court cases in the West Country illustrated yet again that farmers continue to add banned antibiotics and hormones to cattle, pig and poultry feed.

Are these hormones as safe as the Government still claims, despite the ban? Or, as Orville Schell comments in his study of the use of drugs in American livestock production, does our ability to manipulate with both natural and synthetic hormones, however ingenious, also demonstrate 'blindness and hubris'? The latter seems more likely. Schell states:

. . . what is often forgotten is that hormones, substances that are active even in the minutest amounts, are now mass produced and used with an unnerving indiscrimination. Not only are these compounds capable of bringing about the kind of imbalance in the endocrine system . . . but by exciting tissue cells that are sensitive to them, hormones are also able to promote carcinogenesis. The truth is that we still do not know very much about the nature and long term effects of increased burdens of sex hormones.[13]

The most damning evidence against hormones to date is in Puerto Rico, where premature sexual development in young children has been attributed to consumption of hormone-reared chicken. Heart-breaking stories of girls aged five and a half reaching puberty, with some also developing ovarian cysts, have caused outrage and disquiet world-wide. Side-effects are also showing in mature women: there is a higher incidence of uterine and cervical cancer in Puerto Rican women. As with antibiotics, control of the use of hormone growth promoters has always been much more rigorous in the UK than in Puerto Rico, but this does not dispel the general anxiety that the long-term effects of pharmaceuticals added to meat are ultimately unknown and, for the moment, unknowable.

WITHDRAWAL PERIODS

Another large problem created by drug use is inadequate attention to labelling, which results in withdrawal periods (i.e. a period prior to slaughter when the drug should not be administered) being ignored. As one doctor puts it, 'farmers are notorious for not keeping records'.[14] As there is so little control of the administering of antibiotics, a vigorous monitoring system of carcasses is imperative. Yet as we have seen, no such system exists. So reliant is the livestock industry upon pharmaceuticals that some pig farmers actually admit that where there is continuous inclusion of in-feed medicines failure to respect safe with-drawal periods is inevitable. And since most animal feed automatically contains low levels of antibiotics, 'when you have a silo full of medicated food it must be very tempting *not* to fiddle about with a few sacks of unmedicated feed for the animals about to be slaughtered'.[15]

NEW DRUGS

Perhaps the most disturbing aspect of the modern addiction to drug therapy for animals is that now the principle has been firmly accepted drug companies and agricultural-ists alike are constantly pursuing new ways of increasing profits through new compounds. To the drug industry every farming problem is seen as a new challenge to phar-maceutical ingenuity. One common problem, for instance, is that factory farms, with their accumulation of animals in a confined area, are a breeding ground for pests. Toxic chemicals have long been a feature of the fight against this problem and now drug companies have gone further and introduced oral larvicides, mixed into animal feed. The animal digests the chemical which destroys any flies' eggs in the manure. The producers stress that such substances are harmless because only low levels are consumed by the animal and remain in the digestive system for only short periods. Possibly these reassurances are justified. Yet there remains a certain intuitive aversion to the introduction of toxic chemicals over a sustained period into the digestive systems of animals which humans eventually consume.

The drug industry has demonstrated particular interest in the use of prostaglandins, compounds with 'potential to revolutionise the industry'.[16] Minute doses of these powerful substances have the capacity to affect almost every biological function. Once again, exactly how they work remains something of a mystery, but the attraction to farmers is enormous. By administering prostaglandins it is possible to interfere with animals' reproductive systems at almost any point of production. A whole herd of animals can be brought into season at the same time, allowing the stockman to schedule his work almost like any machine operator. Possible other areas of development of this kind of hormonal therapy are chemical castration, bringing all breeding stock to sexual maturity at an earlier age and ovulation stimulation to produce multiple births. Already the labels on some of these prostaglandin therapies warn pregnant women to keep away, adding that 'pregnant women should not even handle the bottles as they could cause abortion and changes in the menstrual cycle ... just through absorption'.[17] Labels on a new synthetic hormone called Regumate introduced by Hoechst (UK) in 1986, go even further. This substance, which acts in the same way as progesterone, carries a warning to the effect that 'it should not be handled by women of child-bearing age and that users should take the precaution of wearing protective gloves and overalls'.[18]

Undeterred by the ban on hormone implants, *Meat Trades Journal* (2nd July 1987) reports that 'science has made sure that there are plenty of new substitutes coming'.[19] Six drug companies are spending $6 million on research and development to bring a 'natural growth hormone' for cattle onto the market. It is reckoned that bovine somatotrophin (BST) will increase milk yields by more than 20%. Such large investment can be justified when it is estimated that BST may be worth $1 billion a year on the commercial market. In the world of big profits from animal exploitation the fact that the EEC already produces far more skimmed milk than it can use is seemingly irrelevant. Milk from cows taking part in trials with the hormone has already found its way into our daily pinta with the backing of the Ministry of Agriculture. Also Beta-agonists, synthetic compounds developed at the Rowett Research Institute in Scotland, 'are already showing themselves capable of inducing leaner carcasses in cattle, sheep, pigs and poultry after being used as in-feed additives'. Other research includes injections of natural growth hormone drawn from the pituitary gland to stimulate quicker growth and addition of 'protected acids' to reduce fat content in the carcass.[20]

ABATTOIRS

A further indication of the disease potential of meat is the high risk among abattoir workers of contracting certain diseases. One-third of all cattle herds in the country suffer from leptospirosis and health officials are concerned that the disease may be passed on to slaughtermen without them knowing it. The problem is that the symptoms are similar to flu and often go unnoticed. The virus can prove dangerous, with major side-effects including meningitis, kidney failure and jaundice.[21] A survey in New Zealand shows that 10% of meat inspectors and 7% of abattoir workers have been infected at some stage. More disturbingly, a report by the American Meat Cutters Union published in the *Journal of Occupational Medicine* lists statistics on the number of its members with cancer and finds 'significant incidents'.[22] The Secretary of the equivalent British union states that his union 'is very concerned about the findings which show significant excesses of bone cancer, cancer of the mouth and cancer of the throat' among employees in abattoirs, bacon factories, meat-processing plants, wholesale meat markets and butchers shops.[22]

Procedures in slaughterhouses also add to the risk of disease. In the words of one environmental health officer, B. Sheard, Deputy Director of Public Health for Amber Valley Council, 'What I believe is causing more salmonella to be found in carcasses is that the speed throughput at the slaughterhouse and the concentration of more slaughtering in big premises is dictating matters'. He calls the procedure 'perhaps satisfactory from the accountant's point of view but certainly not for the public's health'.[23] Careless handling of both carcasses and guts, cross-contamination because of workers cutting successive carcasses with the same knife and methods of slaughter which, for instance, may leave infected faeces splashing onto the carcass in the production of minced pig meat are all common occurrences. In the Autumn of 1986, EEC inspectors surveyed British slaughterhouses and found 'a frightening picture of poor hygiene, slapdash organisation and blood and gore all over the floor'.[24] Production lines running too fast, guts spilled onto the floors, hides touching each other, leading to cross-contamination, lack of cleaning and a general lack of attention to hygiene were all criticized.

THE FINISHED PRODUCT

Environmentally, meat is a natural health hazard. As stated in *Meat Traders Journal*, 'the aroma of freshly cut meat acts as a powerful lure to many unwanted food tasters. Blow flies, blue bottles, green bottles and flesh flies have always found it strongly attractive'.[25] Places where there are large numbers of dead and rotting carcasses are positive palaces for disease-carrying insects. A mixture of meat residues, blood and offal, bones and fat, plus waste-disposal areas and refuse tips in the vicinity of slaughter-houses and butchers shops are large potential breeding sites. Significantly, renderers, who dispose of 1·5 million tonnes of animal waste each year in this country, justify their trade as 'vital to public health',[26] a sure indication of the disease potential of dead animals.

Apart from the health risks associated with conditions in abattoirs, there is the further question of the quality of meat products. Regulations are such that sausages, for instance, may literally include gristle, sinew and rind. The legal definition of lean meat allows a percentage of such delicacies as tail, head, diaphragm and pancreas. Cooked meat products can contain feet, rectum and spinal cord. Many meat products also have their share of 'mechanically recovered meat' (MRM) stripped off the bones by machine after original processing has taken place. Eyeball, nose, lip and snout are among delicacies found in MRM, described by the Government's Food Standards Committee as 'a highly pigmented slurry'.

After television programmes drawing attention to some of these practices, the meat industry has tried hard to dismiss them as untypical. Yet according to their own journal, 'it is common knowledge that in the industry some major companies are using the absence of specific legislation to market low-quality products with names and prices which hardly represent the lowly nature of the contents in the pack'.[27] The *South Yorkshire Trading Standard* conducted a massive survey and found 'a disturbing picture of unacceptable trading practices'.[28] To make matters more complicated, labelling laws encourage the deception. It is perfectly acceptable for MacDonalds and other burger companies to label their foods as '100% pure beef', even though the meat can include significant proportions of, for example, heart, diaphragm, fat, skin, rind, gristle, sinew and other MRM. Pork sausages could include 25% of the head meat from the dead pig, again including gristle and sinew. Minced meat is often up to 30% saturated fat.[28]

Another way of spinning out the profits is to add large quantities of water to the finished product. Injection machines with the capacity to spray water into the carcass from fine needles ensure that weight can be increased. Special salts known as polyphosphates are added to make a water solution which distributes the liquid content more effectively around the dead animal, allowing the liquid to remain in the cells. Although there are no health studies directly linking these salts with human diseases, 'workers dislike using polyphosphates in the factory because they ae known to cause physical reactions'.[29] The *South Yorkshire Trading Standard* enquiry mentioned above found 'excessive levels of added water/curing solution (i.e. polyphosphates) . . . in bacon, ham and other cooked meat'.

Although meat is often advertised as 'natural', it is, in fact, full of additives. An estimated 5% of the total colouring used in our food is found in meat products (though not in fresh meat).[30] Indeed, the meat industry is the colouring manufacturer's second biggest customer in the UK, behind only the soft-drinks trade. The most commonly used colour is red 2G, which has been banned from the USA and the rest of the EEC. An artificial chemical dye made from coal tar, red 2G has been linked with cancers and can cause allergies in children. Tartrazine, also used for colouring, has been associated with hyperactivity in children.

The most popular artificial flavouring added routinely to convenience meats is monosodium glutamate (MSG). MSG's health record is appalling, almost definitely causing side-effects ranging from dizziness and headaches to palpitations. As with all food additives, perhaps more disturbing is the fact that long-term effects on humans are unknown. MSG is often added to pâtés, pies and burgers.

Nitrates are added as a preservative in the production of cured meat. These chemicals have long been suspected of causing cancers, as well as allergies in both adults and children and hypersensitivity in children.[31] Sulphur dioxide finds its way into many meats, including sausages, pies and beefburgers. It acts as a preservative and also makes meat look brighter and fresher. Some studies have linked the substance with irritation of the alimentary tract and it is known to destroy vitamin B1.

Even the retailers of meat are not immune to doctoring the finished product in order to increase desirability to customers. According to consumer journalist Jan Walsh in her book *The Meat Machine*, 'when you buy a joint of meat in a vacuum pack, or a steak say, on a cling film covered tray, you can bet that its colour has been enhanced by gas as well as by clever lighting. Nitrogen, carbon dioxide, oxygen and carbon monoxide are the favourites'.[32]

This then is meat, the substance advertised as the most natural and healthy food for humans. It is difficult to imagine a more inaccurate description for a food that relies upon pharmaceuticals to ensure that animals reach the slaughterhouse alive; kills them in conditions where hygiene standards resemble a poorly maintained public lavatory and then relies upon more chemicals to make the finished product look and taste edible.

CHAPTER FOUR

Is Dairy Produce Good for You?

When first switching from meat to a vegetarian diet most people rely heavily upon dairy produce. Cheese, eggs and milk become the predominant foods, partly because they are familiar and partly because they can be obtained at almost all conventional grocery retailers; also, depending upon dairy produce does not seem quite as foreign or as cranky as basing meals upon nuts, seeds or pulses. Moreover, are we not brought up on the idea that milk is a healthy and natural food, full of goodness? After all, athletes and footballers appear practically to live off their 'daily pinta'. The truth, however, is very different. Dairy produce is suspect both on health and humane grounds. The best policy is to begin your vegetarian diet with as little as you possibly can and to reduce levels progressively.

HEALTH HAZARDS

Farmers Weekly reports 'fat in milk has a very high ratio of saturated to polyunsaturated fat—almost 25:1'.[1] In cheese the ratio is even greater, about 30:1 saturated to polyunsaturated fat (though the fat content in different cheeses does vary considerably). In *The Food Scandal* we learn that our increased intake of dairy foods (also meats) 'now provides the perfect fatty mixture for the development of clogged-up arteries'. Milk, butter, cream and cheese are responsible for 31% of our total fat intake and 41% of our consumption of saturated fat. The conclusion drawn is that 'if it were not for dairy fat, we would all be in better shape'.[2]

Why then has the estimated consumption in the UK roughly doubled in the last 50 years? Like many other dietary disasters, the milk boom probably began with good intentions. As a quick boost for the poor and under-nourished, of whom there were many more 50 years ago, milk did seem an ideal food. It is high in protein and contains a range of vitamins and minerals. Its calcium content is also high and helped to combat diseases of social deprivation, particularly rickets among young children. Yet this does not mean that milk contains any unique qualities. Other food can do the same work as well and at considerably lower cost. As a source of protein, milk contains only about 3% by weight compared with 10% for grains, 20–25% for beans and about 50% for some soya-bean products. As a method of obtaining calcium, it represents an extremely expensive way of obtaining chalk. Sunflower seeds contain at least as much, kale twice as much, sesame seeds about 11 times as much and wakmame and hijiki (sea vegetables) over 13 times as much as milk (per 100 gram edible protein).[3] Recent research has uncovered further that precisely because of the ratio between protein, calcium and fat in cow's milk, any potential benefit is neutralized. Jane Brody in the *New York Times Guide to Personal Health* warns that 'calcium absorption is impaired by excessive dietary fat, and large amounts of animal protein result in an increased loss of calcium through the urine'. In Ms Brody's own words, drinking lots of milk to avoid calcium deficiency 'is like pouring water on a fire to get more heat'.[4]

The price you pay for your bottle on the doorstep may suggest that milk is a cheap food, but that takes no account of the indirect taxes we pay to subsidize its production and storage, the milk lakes to dispose of the surpluses and the research to find new foods which will mop up the unwanted gallons. It is estimated that the cost of storing and disposing of milk takes up about 40% of the total

EEC farm budget. Despite the introduction of a quota system to limit subsidized production, the cost of milk disposal remains a multimillion pound burden on the tax payer. As a result of over-production, milk by-products now also find their way into many food products, household goods and even alcoholic drinks. Dried milk or whey (the watery part of milk that remains after the curds have been removed) are added routinely to commercial goods because they are available at competitively cheap prices to the food industry.

Dairy produce consists of the food designed by nature for female mammals to feed to their young. Each species produces milk especially constituted to suit its own offspring. Cow's milk differs crucially from human milk since it is far richer in protein, minerals and fats. Far from being advantageous to us, these are the precise reasons why it is largely unsuitable for humans. Cow's milk encourages rapid growth in bone and muscle, as you might expect for a large-boned, slow-witted creature which reaches maturity within two years. On the other hand, the greatest early development in humans takes place in the nervous system. Consequently, our milk is perfectly suited to that type of development. It is also higher in vitamin C and D, contains protein that is lighter and more digestible, is sweeter and more alkaline than cow's milk and contains the antibodies necessary to transfer immunity to disease.[3] The differences in the two substances are considerable and suggest why cow's milk has been associated with several diseases among children reared on it. It has been estimated that dairy produce is probably responsible for 75% of all allergies and 40% of digestive disorders in children.[5] If cow's milk is unsuitable for human children, it is obviously not a natural food for adults either. No adult mammal, other than the domestic cat (domesticated by humans) drinks milk after it is weaned. Indeed, an estimated 80% of adults in the world lack the enzyme lactase necessary to digest properly the sugar in milk (25% in the UK).[3] These undigested enzymes are responsible for the formation of mucus and explain why consumers of large amounts of dairy produce often suffer from sinusitis and other 'clogging' complaints. Eczema and asthma are among other diseases associated with milk products, while the quick growth of bone and tissues it provides may also place too much stress upon the organs, particularly the kidneys.

MILK MACHINES

Massive over-production of milk does not deter geneticists from their obsession with increasing productivity. As a result, cows produce almost twice as much milk as they did 30 years ago (approximately 5000 litres per annum) and yields are still increasing. This has not been achieved without the creation of health problems. Huge udders swinging near the ground full of milk are particularly prone to infection. This is especially true when large numbers of animals are confined in a limited space with the subsequent accumulation of dung, as is common in winter quarters for dairy cows. The Ministry of Agriculture estimates from a survey that one-third of cows suffer from the painful udder infection, mastitis, despite routine dosing with antibiotics.

Because of the pressure they are put under to churn out calves every year, together with high quantities of milk, dairy cows now survive an average of only 3·7 lactations. This means they are killed at about five years old, when their natural lifespan is 25–30 years. The reasons for slaughter make depressing reading: 36% are sent to their deaths because of infertility; 24% suffer from a range of unspecified diseases, including metabolic disorders and lameness; another 21% are 'poor yielders'; and 12% are killed because of recurrent mastitis and other disorders. Only 7% die from 'old age'.[6] Old age means that they are no longer able to produce massive amounts of milk and they are packed off or sold at market for slaughter when they have their throats cut so that the last pennyworth of profit can be extracted. Frequently, they are still lactating when the end comes and they are processed for meat pies, canned meats, hamburgers or other convenience food.

It must also be remembered that other meats are a by-product of the dairy industry. In order to produce milk, the cow must give birth once a year, creating a problem of what to do with the unwanted young for whom nature intended the milk. Some calves reared for veal are fattened up for an early death on a diet of milk-substitute gruel (the milk surplus again) despite their craving for more solid food. Others are exported to large veal units abroad, facing long and frightening journeys overseas by sea, air and road before ending up in solitary confinement in a 60 centimetre wide crate in a hot and humid calf house. Death comes after about 14 weeks. The 'luckier' calves are fattened for beef and may live for about 18 months. According to the President of The Scottish Federation of Meat Traders, '80% of European beef comes from dairy cows'.[7] Others replace their mothers in the dairy herd and produce calf after calf until their time for the meat-pie factory arrives too.

Like meat, dairy food is not traditional in many parts of the world. Very little is consumed in the Far East, most of Africa, the Pacific and South America. Rather than a 'natural' food, it is mainly a combination of a powerful dairy industry and inane agricultural policies that are responsible for our overconsumption.

EGG MACHINES

What about eggs? Once again there are health risks involved. Egg yolks are a 'source of cholesterol and fat' and this is why the recommendations of the expert committees, among them NACNE, state that we should eat no more than three or four eggs per week, including those used in cakes, biscuits, desserts and so on.[2]

The cruelties of battery-egg production have received much wider publicity than dairy farming. Few independent observers need convincing that the confinement of hens in cages where they cannot spread their wings is barbaric. Every independent investigation of the battery-cage system in the last decade has condemned it though this has not prevented the industry spreading world-wide. While governments have shown a reluctance to combat inhumane systems of egg production, there is, fortunately, a growing revolt against the cage, leading to increasing numbers of farmers cashing in on a market for free-range eggs. This is a welcome step forward, though some cruelties are an inevitable part of egg production, whatever methods are employed. Approximately 50% of eggs hatched to produce egg-laying hens are male and therefore useless to the egg producer. As we have already seen, millions are killed at a day old, unprotected by law.

The other unavoidable cruelty of free-range production is that, as in battery cages, after only a couple of years the level of egg production goes down to below commercial levels. Although hens have many years of healthy life and good egg laying ahead of them, they are not producing enough profit and are crammed into poultry crates and driven possibly hundreds of miles in whatever weather conditions prevail to the slaughterhouse to face the hideous death described in Chapter 1.

CUTTING DOWN

We can see then that there are many reasons why turning away from a meat-based diet should not mean eating more cheese, eggs or milk products. However, although it is perfectly possible to switch from meat-eating to a life-style which avoids all animal produce, doing without any dairy produce immediately may seem too great a step for some people. Therefore as a guideline, the advice is as follows:

1 Use as little milk, eggs and cheese as you possibly can.
2 On health grounds, skimmed or semi-skimmed milk is preferable to 'ordinary' as it is lower in saturated fats.

3   Most commercial cheeses use animal-based rennet to curdle the milk. This is taken from the stomach of slaughtered calves. Vegetarian cheddar, where the rennet is produced from vegetable produce, is available from most health-food shops and one or two supermarkets, although it is more expensive.

4   When you do buy eggs, make sure that they are free range. There are other systems, such as barn eggs, but although these are better than battery cages, they often involve large numbers of birds in a very small area. They cannot be recommended.

5   Margarine or butter? Butter is high in saturated fats; margarines vary in their ratio of saturated to unsaturated. The labelling is such that it is often hard to distinguish which margarines contain least numbers of harmful substances, but as a general rule look for the wording 'high in polyunsaturates'. Some margarines contain animal fats, so you must also look out for 'made of 100% vegetable oils'. Unfortunately, to make life even more complicated, even those that do say that they are made of 100% 'vegetable oils' and 'high in polyunsaturates' usually contain some dairy produce (most often whey). Already there are several margarines that are totally free from animal produce on the market and they are mostly available from health food shops: Granose vegetable and sunflower margarines, Vitaqull and Vitaseig both imported from West Germany, Meridian and Suma sunflower margarines are the most readily available. Safeways Pure is one of the first vegan spreads to find its way onto supermarket shelves. It is probably true to say that neither margarine nor butter is good for you. Margarines are simply hardened fat with added colour, flavouring, emulsifiers and vitamins. Butter, as we pointed out, is high in saturated fat. Whichever you do decide to buy, use as little as you possibly can. Good wholemeal bread does not need layers of fat to make it interesting.

6   Wherever possible, cook with oil instead of margarine.

49

Cooking oil is one food for which you should be prepared to pay for a good quality brand. It is not enough simply to buy a bottle marked 'vegetable oils' because these may be predominantly palm oil and high in saturated fats. It is much better to go to the local health-food store and buy sunflower, soya, corn or safflower oil. In addition, if you can afford it, you should purchase an oil marked 'unrefined' and/or 'cold-pressed'. This indicates that the oil has been extracted from the plant with as little adulteration as possible. Apart from the health advantages, these oils give a delicious taste to your vegetables or whatever else you might choose to cook in them.

THE NON-ANIMAL DAIRY

In the guidelines above we have begun to tackle the problem which many potential converts must be asking. Namely, if I cut down on dairy produce, what should I put in its place? Our next task is to take some of the most common uses of dairy foods and to suggest some alternatives.

Milk

There are now numerous brands of soya milk available. They vary in taste and also taste considerably different from cow's or goat's milk. Some people prefer the taste; others like soya milk after getting used to them and breaking the habit of a lifetime of drinking cow's milk. A minority simply do not like them at all. The best advice is to persevere for a while, because it may simply be that your taste-buds take time to adjust. Both because of the increasing numbers of vegans and the numbers allergic to cow's milk, there is a growing market for soya milks and the taste seems to be improving all the time. Most of them do contain sugar although there are non-sweetened varieties too. With one exception, soya milk comes in ready-to-drink cartons, the exception being that distributed by Plamil Foods Ltd, who produce a concentrated drink to be diluted with water or used undiluted as 'cream'. Most soya milks provide the same amount of protein as a cup of cow's milk, with the bonus of containing one-third less calories from fat and none from cholesterol.[8] Other vegans prefer to take their drinks black and their breakfast cereals with fruit juice.

Sauces
Soya milk can also be used in all sauces.

Cheese
A 'cheese' can be made by adding four ounces of soya flour to four ounces of heated margarine, with yeast extract to taste and then refrigerating. It has to be admitted that it does not taste much like English cheddar! 'Cream cheeses' can also be made from tofu, while Plamil Foods Ltd have become the first commercial company to introduce a non-dairy 'cheese spread', named Veeze.

Sandwiches
In place of cheese, try peanut butter (many companies include sugar in their peanut butter but those on sale in health-food shops and some supermarkets do not), tahini (spread made from ground sesame seeds), yeast extract or sunflower-seed spread. Several non-animal pâtés are also available. Add fresh salad and/or bean sprouts.

Eggs
We are brought up on the idea that eggs are necessary for binding many savoury dishes and also for producing cakes and biscuits. This is a fallacy. Vegan cook books show that eggs can easily be replaced. To give only two examples here, oats and water in a nut roast will bind the meal together or a little fruit juice can replace eggs in some cakes. Sarah Brown's recipes include a vegan nut roast, a cake and quiche made without eggs.

Yoghurt
You can make your own. A yoghurt culture can be bought from many health-food shops and this can be fed daily with soya milk. Sojal were the first firm to launch a non-dairy yoghurt, called Yoga in natural, raspberry and strawberry flavours. It is available from health-food shops, as are White Wave vegan yoghurts.

Ice Cream
Several non-dairy alternatives now exist, the most economical being Vive, which can be purchased from Sainsbury's. Health-food shops are also stocking non-dairy ice cream. They are often expensive but delicious.

Milk Shakes
Soya milk now also comes in different flavours, ideal as milk-shake alternatives. Granose Ltd markets soya milks in strawberry, coconut and raspberry. A small amount of juice concentrate mixed with soya milk produces a delicious thick 'milk shake'.

This is not a cookbook and those who wish to pursue the non-animal replacements for dairy foods further than the few recipes in Part 2 can purchase one of several new vegan cookbooks on the market. Reference should also be made to Chapter 11. The purpose of this brief summary is simply to show that it is possible to replace animal products in the diet without any difficulty.

CHAPTER FIVE

Human Hunger

Harrowing scenes on television in October 1984 of human hunger in Ethiopia and the Sudan prompted more people than ever before to think of and even to act upon the problems of starvation. With their record in November 1984 and concert in July 1985, Band Aid achieved enormous success in raising both public money and concern, while other Third World charities also received massive public support in response to the horror of hunger, grief and death.

Without wishing to detract at all from these acts of human generosity, the point cannot be stressed too greatly that it is not enough simply to give money in times of extreme crisis. Human starvation is a daily occurrence in many parts of the world, regardless of the presence or absence of television cameras. Although many of the causes seem outside our influence, being associated with inept politicians or inhospitable climates, it does not follow that individuals living in the Western World are absolved from any greater responsibility than handing over their cash. We all have something to offer because any long-term solutions to problems in Africa and Asia demand fundamental changes in life-styles enjoyed by most of us in the rich half of the world. Almost all of us consume more than our fair share of the world's resources.

As I sit in my comfortable chair with a secure roof over my head and good food in the kitchen it is all too easy to offer neat summaries of the fearful problems of aid and starvation. The following oversimplified categories are intended only as a useful outline to some of the choices we face in striving to alleviate the worst excesses of human hunger.

1 Emergency food aid

Although vital in times of extreme famine caused by natural disasters or war, emergency aid does not offer any long-term solutions. On the contrary, at other times it can be detrimental to the interest of Third World economies by destroying whatever stability exists. When markets are flooded with cheap food, the livelihood of local producers is often destroyed. If at all possible, it is much more beneficial to spend funds on trying to minimize dangers before they can escalate into disasters.

2 Introduction of Western technology and agricultural methods into Third World nations

Far too much of our current aid is of this nature. It is normally inappropriate because poor nations: (a) cannot afford to maintain such capital intensive systems; (b) lack technological skills to build and service them without becoming dependent on donor countries; and (c) such methods rely on technology rather than labour and consequently they do not create employment for hungry people.

3 Development of Third World agriculture by introducing technology appropriate to the needs and state of progress in the receiving nation

Again this in itself is a massive subject. To put it crudely, it means ensuring that basic necessities are freely available, particularly water for irrigation and drinking and simple tools and techniques for farming. In other words, it means agricultural technology which can be understood and utilized by local people in poorer nations in order to improve both the quality of their soil and the quantity of cultivatible land. This way it should be possible to increase yields, particularly of staple food crops.

4 Begin with ourselves

By altering our own life-styles we can attempt to no longer consume more than our fair share of the world's resources. Whilst this may not have any noticeable immediate effect, its great value in the long-term is that it will give poorer nations example worthy of imitation. It is a myth to suppose that the way *we* live is of no influence to decision-makers in the Third World, because it is inevitable that they will be impressed by *our* comfort and lack of poverty. It can easily be overlooked that our wasteful habits are unsustainable. The importance of utilizing our own resources more efficiently and responsibly is, perhaps, best illustrated by the statistic that the USA with only 6% of the world's population, consumes 35% of the world's resources.[1] If we take Ghandi's maxim, 'The world has enough for every man's need but not enough for every man's greed', we in the West, are greedy.

The relevance of vegetarianism to both the third and fourth points cannot be overestimated because the world cannot afford agricultural systems like ours, which depend upon massive consumption of animal produce. Meat production is a very inefficient way of producing food. As Figures 5.1 and 5.2 illustrate, it is far less wasteful, both in terms of energy and protein, to grow food directly for human consumption. This is because most of the food fed to animals in order to fatten them is wasted in their digestion, cell replacement and other functions. Consequently, if we are to increase the possibility of feeding a growing world population, we have to rely increasingly upon vegetarian food and not waste land growing feed for animals.

THE GRAIN DRAIN

When we relate this fact to our eating habits in the rich half of the world we can see that we are both squanderous of resources and that our diets actually contribute to famine among others less fortunate. If we include grass-

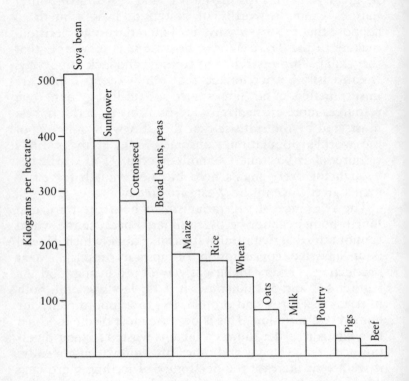

Figure 5·1 Protein yields (kilogram per hectare) from various crops.
Source: The Vegetarian Society (UK) Ltd.

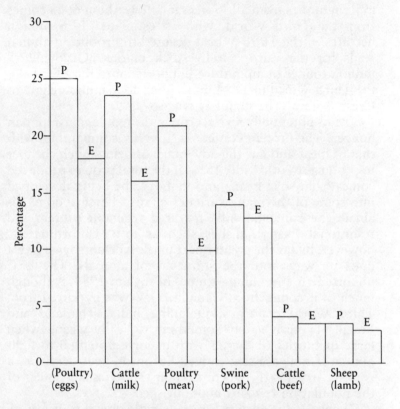

Figure 5·2 Protein and energy conversion efficiency. Percentage obtained in relation to input. Note that the maximum per cent is well below 30%. P = protein yield from the product as a percentage of protein consumed; E = energy obtained from the product as a percentage of energy consumed.

lands, in the UK alone more than 90% of agricultural land is used to grow feed for animals. In addition, we actually import food for the same purpose. The EEC is the largest buyer of animal feeds in the world—nearly 40 million tonnes from all sources in 1984. About 60% comes from the Third World, with an estimated 14·6 million hectares in the Third World devoted to producing animal feeds for the European livestock market. Of the 22·5 million tonnes of animal feed imported into the EEC from the Third World in 1984, more than four million came to Great Britain. The majority was soya.[2]

Soya is potentially a vital crop in the fight against human hunger. The protein content is 'roughly comparable' with that of meat and has the advantage of being much cheaper to produce. Worldwide, 15% of the total protein produced comes from soya beans and it should be being developed into some of the many varieties of soya-based food available.[3] These include milk, textured vegetable protein and traditional Eastern dishes such as tofu. Unfortunately, however, by far the greater part of the world's soya harvest finds its ways into the stomachs of animals. The EEC imported 16 434 million tonnes of soya in 1984. Although much of it comes from Canada, 53% was imported from Third World countries, including India, Thailand and Brazil.[2] There is surely something radically wrong when large quantities of a crop with massive potential to fight human famine are sent to feed European livestock from a country like Brazil, where Oxfam estimates that 60% of the population remains malnourished.

Of course, the answer is not a simple one of transferring the soya from animals to people, because the vast quantities being grown in poorer countries is, itself a result of exploitation of people. Multinational companies have bought vast areas of land to fuel the animal-feed industry and have removed the possibility of peasants sustaining themselves on traditional food crops. So while the potential for soya is undeniable, it can only benefit the poor when seen as part of an overall policy of agricultural expansion which respects the rights of poorer people to own land on which they also can grow their traditional food crops.

Criminally, other imported animal feed comes from nations with even greater problems than Brazil. It seems incredible that in the 12 months dating from September 1983, when famine was already a massive problem, we actually bought more than £1.5 million worth of linseed cake, cottonseed cakes and rape-seed meal from Ethiopia.[4] Admittedly, none of this food could have been eaten directly by humans, but it does mean that good quality agricultural land is being wasted on growing animal feed for export rather than food for hungry people. Alas it is the same story in many areas of the Third World. World-wide over 450 million tonnes—more than one-third of the food grains produced—are fed to livestock, while at the same time an estimated 500 million people are severely malnourished.[5]

From these figures the message is clear. It has been estimated that in Great Britain alone we could sustain a population of roughly 250 million people on an all-vegetarian diet, whereas at the moment we are hopelessly dependent upon imported feed to maintain our animal-based agriculture. Meanwhile, even to meet current levels of consumption, we are 'totally underproduced in most vegetables'[6] and the profitability of our cereal crop depends wholly upon intensive animal farms (with over half the UK production being fed to animals)[7] and EEC subsidies for storage and disposal. Latest projections suggest that the EEC grain mountain could reach 80 million tonnes by 1990. This can hardly be called a model of agricultural efficiency for the poor to follow.

MORE POULTRY MEANS MORE HUMAN HUNGER

Yet, inevitably, follow is what Third World countries are doing. Often they are manipulated into doing so by

Western governments and business concerns looking for export markets regardless of the inappropriateness of their goods for the economies of receiving nations. All too often, entrepreneurs or corrupt governments in developing nations are only too ready to buy. As a result, we have seen dramatic increases in the spread of animal farming in Africa and Asia, particularly that of battery hens and broiler chickens. In the fight against hunger this is indefensible because grain has first to be found to feed the poultry who then waste most of the food value before being slaughtered. Even after slaughter the poultry can never help the poorer people because there is no possibility of them being able to afford to purchase such an expensive luxury.

In the circumstances it is criminal that in Africa, for instance, there has been a 98% increase in poultry production since 1975.[8] Never satisfied, the poultry industry continues to emphasize the potential for growth in the area, pointing out that the African population has increased by over 100 million in the last five years.[8] In fact, such an increase in population is an added reason why factory farming is dangerously inappropriate. If there are more and more mouths to feed, how can you afford to squander land on growing food for animals? By the early 1980s, ten million tonnes of grain were being imported annually by African nations, constituting the cereal consumption of one in five of the entire population of the continent.[9] If the poultry industry continues to expand, this figure is bound to increase and so is the problem of malnutrition.

Already the destructive consequences of intensive poultry farming are becoming apparent in many nations. In Nigeria, a country with a poultry industry of some 40 million birds, the factory-farming system is on the verge of collapse because of a short supply of maize, groundnut cake, soya meal, fish meal, vitamins and minerals to feed the chickens during drought and failed harvest.[10] If there is no food for humans, chickens are not much help to the hungry. Unfortunately, the same agricultural systems are being adapted by practically every Third World state from Bangladesh to Sudan, from India to Tanzania. Perhaps most criminally of all, Ethiopia is now expanding its factory farming. Already there are 500 000 broiler chickens being fattened there and at the height of the famine the Government announced targets 'of two million'. There are also plans for battery-egg farms with 200 000 birds in both Assmara and Eritrea.[11]

An Ethiopian Government spokesman claims that the purpose of this expansion is 'to provide minimum requirements of protein to the people'.[11] Incredibly, the same spokesman goes on to say that soya beans have recently been introduced into Ethiopia and that 'our ultimate objective is to develop the production of corn and soya'[11] to feed chickens. How much more sensible it would be to introduce the simple technology which could utilize the full potential of the soya bean, producing milk, flour and some of the highly nutritious foods of the Far East.

If we take into account the protein value that is lost in the conversion from grain to meat and the exceptionally high mortality rates that occur when underdeveloped nations like Ethiopia undertake highly sophisticated factory-farm systems (between 20% and 30% of birds fattened in Ethiopia die before they reach the slaughterhouse and are, therefore, inedible[11]), approximately 20 times more protein would be available for the people. Moreover, the hungry are more likely to be able to afford cheap soya than high priced chicken, though it has to be admitted that with the present disasters affecting many parts of Africa and Asia, even soya beans are too luxurious a crop for the poorest areas. Millet, maize and other grains are traditionally cheaper to grow.

The development of animal farming, particularly factory farming, in both Africa and Asia, represents another major threat to hungry people. Rather than providing humans with food, farm animals compete with us. The poultry industry freely admits this. Bemoaning the difficulties of finding adequate sources of animal feed in Africa, a spokesman is quoted as saying that 'East and West Africa have abundant fish generally used for human consumption but quite easily diverted to animal feed use'.[12] In other words, fish are diverted from the hungry to feed the rich.

THE REAL WAY FORWARD

Traditionally poorer nations rely almost exclusively upon vegetarian food because they cannot afford to throw away valuable grains for fattening animals. The food staples are crops like rice and lentils in India, millet, maize, cassava and beans and vegetables in Africa and chick peas and wheat in the Middle East. Similar foods have maintained Third World cultures for centuries. It must, therefore, make sense for agricultural aid to be based upon improving the food-producing potential of these existing crops, making the most of the resources already available. Despite the destructive trend towards factory farming, there are one or two encouraging examples of what can be achieved. In Niger, for example, a project partly funded by Oxfam has helped to dig wells and provide tools and seed to small farmers for vegetable gardening. This has enabled many families to survive despite the problems of prolonged drought in this part of Africa. Similarly, in contrast to the idiocy of factory farming, Oxfam in Ethiopia are helping to dig wells, build irrigation channels, terrace land and plant trees; they are also putting in supplies of good clean water and buying tools and seeds.[13]

Perhaps the most promising new approach, however, is the promotion of leaf-protein projects. One major scheme has been in Sri Lanka, where the British-based organization Find Your Feet has been working with the Sri Lankan self-help education group Sarvodya.[14] A simple technology has been developed to pulp large amounts of leaves. The strained juice is then heated until it curdles, strained again to separate the curd from the liquor and then the curd is pressed in muslin. Surprisingly, the result is a high quality food, higher in protein than many seeds and pulses, including soya, and also containing considerable amounts of iron and Beta-Carotene—both valuable in helping to combat and prevent malnutrition. In the Sri Lankan project, leaf protein is added to coconut and rice water to produce a liquid containing nutrients resembling those found in milk. A drink of the 'leaf soup', known locally as Kola Kenda, is fed daily to pre-school children in nursery schools set up by Sarvodya. This provides one-third of their daily protein requirements. Significant improvements in the height and weight of the children have been noted since the project began in 1985.

Other projects with leaf protein have begun in Mexico, India and Ghana. Hundreds of green leaves are edible and suitable for leaf-concentrate production in many parts of the world. It gives 'a greater yield of protein per hectare than any other crop'.[15] This method of food production seems particularly appropriate to many problem areas in the Third World. Often, though not always of course, leaves are available in abundance and the technology to utilize them is cheap, simple and easy to maintain, thus encouraging self-reliance. Although the finished product may not sound very appetizing compared with our highly sophisticated Western habits, leaf protein is a high-quality food, uninteresting in itself, but easily incorporated into existing recipes and certainly better than nothing in times of severe famine.

In contrast, the overall picture in the Third World is not very promising. More often than not, the foods that we are prescribing for Third World nations create more health problems than cures. In the words of Professor James of the Rowett Research Institute:

> ... we are already storing up a time bomb in Africa. Cases of high blood pressure in West and South Africa are now increasing at a terrifying rate. If they go on like this, by the year 2000 it will be the largest single budgeting drain on their health sector and in the West

we are largely to blame, by sending the wrong sort of food aid and exporting totally inappropriate forms of agriculture.[16]

A report in the journal *Nutrition and Health*, published in 1983, states that in Africa, 'the bean is coming to be despised in the growing fashion for meat.[17]

Of course it would be unreasonable to blame all the problems of food production in the Third World solely on factory farming and the increase in meat eating, but it is no accident that the tremendous escalation in broiler and battery-hen farming and the introduction of Western 'fast food' generally has coincided with mounting problems. One-hundred-and-fifty million Africans in 24 countries now face hunger and malnutrition while even those who can afford to eat well are becoming increasingly prone to Western diseases. To make any long-term impression on the terrible and growing problems of human hunger in developing nations it is vital that we set an example here in the West by using our own land resources responsibly. Vegetarian diets meet this requirement and also have the added advantage of encouraging compassion rather than barbarism. At the moment, our affluent habits teach only waste and violence.

CHAPTER SIX

A Greener World

Small quantities of animal produce can be consumed without damaging human health or our potential to fight hunger in the Third World. The case for total vegetarianism must rest only on the grounds that it is morally unacceptable to kill animals for food. The main argument is simple: we do not need to indulge in the miseries of meat production because there is no reason why human beings have to eat the flesh of other creatures in order to live a satisfying life. As this statement is undeniable, wherein lies the justification? Since pleasure is the most valid defence put forward for flesh consumption, is it not time to accept the viewpoint stated forcefully by Australian-born philosopher Peter Singer?

In an early stage of our development most human groups held to a tribal ethic. Members of the tribe were protected, but people of other tribes could be robbed or killed as one pleased. Gradually the circle of protection expanded, but as recently as 150 years ago we did not include blacks. So African human beings could be captured, shipped to America and sold. In Australia white settlers regarded aborigines as a pest and hunted them down, much as kangaroos are hunted down today. Just as we have progressed beyond the blatantly racist ethic of the era of slavery and colonialism, so we must now progress beyond the speciesist ethic of the era of factory farming, of the use of animals as mere research tools, of whaling, seal hunting, kangaroo slaughter and

the destruction of wilderness. We must take the final
step in expanding the circle of ethics.[1]

IS VEGETARIAN AGRICULTURE A REAL POSSIBILITY?

Even allowing that a totally vegetarian society will not
occur in the Western World within the lifetime of anybody
living today (unless prompted by a disaster of unthinkable
proportions), the question of whether it is a practical
possibility or simply an abstraction divorced from real
understanding of life does have some relevance. Certainly,
non-vegetarians often seem obsessed by the search for a
clinching argument which will invalidate all other forceful
reasons why we might avoid animal products. Most
vegetarians will be familiar with the kind of questions I
mean: How about desert tribes or eskimos who live solely
by hunting and fishing and do not appear to have alternative sources of food available? What could be used in
order to maintain soil fertility if there were no animal
manure available? What would happen to all farm
animals? What would happen if rabbits or other 'pests'
savage crops? Would the countryside not turn into a vast,
featureless prairie with wildlife destroyed? These are
among the most familiar queries.

It has to be admitted that it is difficult to find complete
answers to some of these questions. The case of the
eskimos does indicate strongly that at some stages of
human development in some areas, it may be necessary for
people to kill animals in order to survive. Other problems,
although not insurmountable, do suggest solutions that
may seem so radical at the present time as to invite ridicule
from the lay person. Animal wastes, for instance, are not
required to maintain soil fertility: the important factor is
to return all waste to the land. A combination of green
manure techniques and the recycling of human waste
should be perfectly adequate. The technology to treat the
latter could easily be developed further. It would be far

more beneficial to return some of our sewage to the soil rather than dump it all into the sea to pollute our beaches and oceans. Any cultural 'taboo' about using human effluent is simply irrational. Why should animal manure, supposedly from 'inferior creatures', be acceptable and human manure not?

Farm animals would survive because a vegetarian agricultural system would allow ample space for nature reserves where animals could graze and root freely, until, in time, the more hardy and traditional species could perhaps even revert to their feral state. Obviously though, you could not allow the present numbers reared for meat and milk to survive, nor would it be either sensible or desirable to do so. The genetic mutations that we now rear in factory farms have been designed solely to put on weight quickly and as a result they suffer injuries and illness from the unnatural strain put upon their limbs and organs. There would be no rhyme nor reason for these breeds to continue, for to perpetuate them would be only to perpetuate suffering.

'Pests' will, it is true, always bring some problems, however well balanced your system of food production, though infinitely greater care could be taken to control without resort to poison or snares. Apart from the traditional virtues of strong fencing and annual crop rotation to ensure that 'pests' do not find themselves permanently in the same amenable environment, there are possibilities of repulsion through sonar systems or learning sufficiently about the reproductive cycle of animals and insects in order to apply forms of contraceptive baits. (Obviously, the introduction of any such treatment would have to be understood very fully beforehand to be certain that it would affect only target species.) Above all, every effort should be made to minimize problems before they occur. Pest control is another area where prevention is always better than cure. *Veterinary Record* states:

Today it is being realised that preventive management

of potential pest species is often more logical, cost effective and humane. The use of repellents or barriers, changing farming practices, modifying a pest animal's breeding capability and providing alternative sources of food to attract the pest away from its target may all be efficient methods of finding long term solutions to pest problems.[2]

As far as conservation is concerned, a vegetarian world should diminish the problems of wildlife destruction and pollution of the environment. As I have indicated in Chapter 5, it takes considerably more land to grow food for pasture animals than it does to grow food for direct human consumption. It has been estimated that it would be possible to grow enough cereals, beans, nuts and vegetables to feed the current population of the UK on only approximately one-third of our agricultural land.[3] This leads to the obvious conclusion that the nearer we move towards a vegetarian world, the less land we would need to grow food and the more areas would be available for other purposes, including conservation.

As long ago as 1970, Professor Ingram from the Meat Research Institute was informing his audience that 'the yields of protein per unit area even from the waste of conventional cropping, could apparently be far more than conventional animal production and might be converted with insignificant losses into food directly consumable by humans'.[4] In answer to those who might 'regard such a prospect as horrible', Professor Ingram added the pertinent remark that 'I doubt whether those people ever handled dung, or worked in a slaughterhouse'.

A VEGETARIAN FUTURE

The arguments for a vegetarian agriculture normally meet with several objections. First, when thinking about an agricultural system based upon vegetarianism, people tend to think in terms of what we have now and to imagine vast, hedgeless, prairie-like fields of barley, or else mile after mile of ugly greenhouses. Even if this were the case, we must re-emphasize that such a system would still result in less rather than more land being utilized than at present. More importantly, cereals and intensive horticulture would only be part of a vegetarian world. As far as possible, the aim would be to utilize a mixed rotational system, with hedgerows and tree stands breaking up the areas of cultivation. Artificial inputs would also be abandoned eventually.

As well as a variety of cereals (wheat, oats, barley, rye, buckwheat, durum wheat, etc.), fruits, vegetables and nuts (there is some scope for walnuts, pine- and cob-nuts in certain areas of this country), we should also be examining the potential of novel forms of food—from green-leaf vegetables to lupins, sunflowers and other forms of protein. Rape-seed, lupins and sunflowers are also a valuable source of oil and have the additional benefit of being nitrogen-fixing plants, fertilizing the land in order to nourish next year's crop. Commercial lupin growing in the UK has already reached an early stage of development. At the moment, the crop is grown exclusively for animal feed, but its potential for human food is widely recognized as an alternative to soya 'readily acceptable . . . in a range of food items'.[5] Sunflowers, it has to be admitted, still create a problem because there is a need to perfect an early maturing variety before they can be considered as a viable commercial crop in the UK. Nevertheless, there seems no reason why such seeds cannot be obtained if given priority by researchers. Already *Farmers Weekly* reports that 'the race is on' and that trials are now taking place. Once established, sunflowers 'get good results with few inputs'.[6]

As the desirability for greater quantities of plant protein is recognized and development grants are given largely to support a vegetarian system of agriculture, then the range of food sources would increase dramatically. Currently, 70% of the world's food is obtained from only 20 staples.

The unexplored possibilities of other potential food crops is limitless. New Era Foods, for example, have already given us some indication of how we might use myco-protein, a fungus grown on glucose derived from starch. This can be prepared to give many alternative textures from 'meat-like' chunks to powders utilized in biscuit production. Myco-protein also has the advantage of being low in fat and cholesterol-free, yet high in protein and dietary fibre.'[7]

The idea of a diet including some 'strange' items as staples may, at first, seem outrageous. So is a vegetarian world mere fantasy? Professor Watkin Williams, from the Department of Agricultural Botany at the University of Reading, spells out the possibilities:

> National food requirements based only on crop production could be provided from half of the present yield per acre—the yield level in the early part of this century when no artificial nitrogen was applied. In this way 500 000 tonnes of elemental nitrogen and 1 000 000 litres of oil would be saved. Clearly, an exercise such as this highlights the heavy price we pay, in terms of both *resources for land and support energy*, for a meat diet. Sooner rather than later, this price may be recognised as *too high*.[8] (My emphasis).

Against this, some ecologists would protest that animal production is also responsible for some of the most valued features of our English countryside, particularly hay and pasture meadows. At best, this argument is less than half-valid, because areas of natural pasture are already fast disappearing. In fact, it is mostly animal farming that is responsible for the loss of our hedgerows, down- and heathland, woods, ponds, streams and flower-rich meadows, with areas being consistently ploughed up for sowing intensive grasses or cereals. More than half of the cereals grown in the UK go for animal feed and almost the total intensive grass production fuels intensive livestock-keeping. Neither is capable of sustaining our wild birds, flowers or animals. Indeed, these very developments led Marion Shoard, in her courageous book *The Theft of the Countryside*,[9] to conclude that the English landscape is under sentence of death.

It has to be admitted that a switch to growing food for direct human consumption would result in radical changes to our landscape; the point is, however, that the overall balance should prove beneficial to the environment. Inevitably, a world that had accepted a system of food production based upon non-violence to animals would insist that the vast areas no longer needed to produce food were treated with the respect which would protect and encourage our flora and fauna. What sort of world would it be? Even allowing for other areas of development (industry, housing, etc.) more than adequate space would remain for recreation (e.g. national parks) and for the development of wildlife reserves. Areas of natural pasture might lose their utility, but could still be maintained for conservation purposes. Small numbers of 'farm animals' could themselves graze there, preventing a return to scrub as they live their lives free from factory farms and slaughterhouses. We could also devote greater areas of uplands to forestry, again diminishing our need for artificial energy sources. Compared to other EEC nations, Great Britain has very few tree plantations, with only 7% of our land turned over to forestry compared to the average of 20%. It is estimated that we could produce all our required liquid fuels from 17% of the UK land area and all our gas from 15%. Whether or not total self-sufficiency is desirable, it is evident that an increase in areas of forestry would be beneficial to our natural resources.

Worldwide, the protection of forests is a particularly urgent problem. They are disappearing fast, the main cause being the vast areas felled for animal farming. In Central America, the introduction of bulldozers to fell trees so that cattle can be grazed (in order to provide beef for the USA hamburger industry) is one of the worst modern examples of short-term greed causing long-term disaster. When we destroy forests, we do not simply kill off the habitat and thereby threaten the existence of many wild creatures and plants, we also interfere with levels of oxygen in the atmosphere and with the climate (the relation between the sun and land is altered, disturbing air currents). More disturbingly, we cause soil erosion and floods:

> Forests encourage rainfall, both by releasing water vapour and by forcing saturated air to rise over them and condense. When rain falls it is checked firstly by the leaves and then by the roots which regulate the rate of run-off into streams and rivers. When tree cover is removed rain attacks in torrents, washing away precious top soil, which has taken centuries to form. Afterwards, the earth is soon baked dry again. A pattern of flood and drought becomes inevitable. In hot climates once fertile land is turned into desert, bringing the misery of famine.[10]

It is worth reminding ourselves that overgrazing has been one of the chief causes of creating deserts over the centuries.

WATER ISN'T EVERYWHERE

A switch to vegetarianism would also help to conserve other natural resources, particularly water supplies. Water is a gift we take for granted in the West. We see the devastating effects of drought in Third World countries, yet, with our supplies always on tap, it is difficult for us to consider shortages in any terms other than a ban on garden hoses during exceptionally dry summers! Yet ecologists are constantly warning us that we should never unnecessarily waste our supplies. In the long term, we cannot afford to allow millions of farm animals to compete with us for drinking water, any more than we can let them waste any other of the earth's resources. It has been estimated that it takes 273 litres of water to produce 450 grams of wheat and 1136.5 litres to produce 450 grams of rice compared to a minimum of 9092 and a maximum of 27,276 litres to produce 450 grams of meat. Slaughterhouses alone consume an obscene quantity of water for washing away blood and guts, with chicken-processing plants responsible for up to 454 million litres every day—enough to supply the needs of 25 000 humans. Worldwide, livestock are responsible for consuming 80% of water supplies.[11] In the rich half of the world we may find that price far 'too high' in the future: in the Third world, these figures represent another compelling reason why increased meat production must be opposed immediately.

The principal reason why ecologists in the Western world are so concerned with maintaining adequate supplies of drinking water is the damage caused by pollution. When most people think of water pollution, they probably imagine industrial waste or else the seeping of nitrates from fertilizers into supplies. Yet, serious as these problems are, it is probably modern methods of animal farming which remain the chief source of water pollution in the UK. The trade magazine *Dairy Farmer* states that 'farming has caused a great deal of water pollution, resulting in the death of many thousands of fish and the contamination of water supplies over large areas'.[12] The problem is increasing. 'As well as the more noticeable cases', *Dairy Farming* continues, 'in which great slugs of effluent move downstream carrying all before them, there could be a more serious problem of continual trickles of slurry gradually altering the water content'. The article ends with the warning that water can only cope with surprisingly low levels of pollution and that 'in many cases' we could be 'storing up serious problems for the future'. Although there are laws governing the distribution of wastes into rivers and streams, they are failing to control the accumulation of untreated effluent containing residues of antibiotics and other drugs, hormones, parasites and other disease pathogens, plus slaughterhouse waste from 500 million farm animals a year. Heavy pollution from slaughterhouses includes fat and inedible offal, as well as 118 million litres of blood shed every year[11] (enough to fill 260 average-sized swimming pools), half of which goes down the drains. Several farms and slaughterhouses have been prosecuted for polluting local waters in recent years, including the infamous 'bootiful' Bernard Matthews turkey enterprise in Norfolk and The Milk Marketing Board in Gloucestershire.

The warning signs of where this unheeding pollution might lead are already visible in some parts of Europe. In the Netherlands, it is estimated that nitrate levels are so high that within 10–20 years there will be no water available for drinking. All water used for drinking will have to be imported. Moroever, the damage is long term: in the South and East Netherlands it will be hundreds of years before water can be drunk again. The damage is caused by the massive amounts of manure produced by intensive chicken and pig houses and dairy herds. Such vast amounts have found their way into the soil that the smell alone is killing trees. The manure is also devastating the soil, partly because of the excess ammonia and partly because the slurry from factory farming is too thin and watery for the soil to absorb in large quantities. Consequently, the slurry has seeped into the water-table. In addition to nitrates, the slurry also contains antibiotics, and minerals such as zinc and phosphorous. The problem has reached these disastrous levels because of both the flat landscape and the vast number of intensively farmed animals in a small area. It would surely be foolish to imagine that Great Britain could avoid similar catastrophe in certain areas (notably Humberside and certain parts of East Anglia) before too long.

Meat production wastes and pollutes. 'Energy and water requirements for animal production are between 10 and 1000 times greater than they would be for an equal amount of plant food'. These facts have led Professor Williams from the University of Reading to conclude that 'a greater proportion of the diet in industrialised countries will have to be derived from plant products. There is now no other way in which world supplies of primary products, including energy, can meet the pressure of mouths to feed'.[13]

THE SPIRIT THAT COULD BRING CHANGE

The point of all this is not to establish some cast-iron theory about the feasibility of a vegetarian world. No mature vegetarian would ever claim to have all the answers. Rather, what needs to be established is that all manner of things do become possible, provided that we utilize all human knowledge and technical ingenuity towards discovering the least violent methods of confronting agricultural problems. It is very simple to pick holes in any idyllic concept of how the world might be in the distant future. If an eighteenth-century agriculturist had come up with the idea of our current methods, he would surely have been declared insane! What is much more vital is the spirit which vegetarianism represents. It is this spirit which the present age needs desperately, for if we accept Ghandi's statement that 'the greatness of a nation and its progress can be judged by the way its animals are treated' then the Western World in the 1980s has almost infinite room for improvement.

Against a world which seems ready to inflict almost any indignity on other creatures for its own greed, vegetarianism is one important manifestation of the human spirit struggling to create a world where compassion and respect dominate profit and destruction and where the convenience of chemical poisons and factory farms is abandoned in favour of a new belief in treating every difficulty which arises with the least violent and wasteful approach imaginable. Realistically, it is not always possible to avoid killing—drive a vehicle on

summer nights and moths will fly into your headlights*—
and sometimes humans do have to struggle for their own
space in the natural world as does every other living creature. Nevertheless, a belief in not killing animals simply
to satisfy our own taste-buds is part of a deep-rooted
challenge to the will to destroy which plagues humanity.
More than refusing to eat animal flesh, it means accepting
the responsibility of 'living without cruelty' as far as it is
possible to do so and having the courage to inconvenience
ourselves in pursuit of that goal.

* Of course, concern for the environment should also
encourage responsible use of transport facilities, particularly
minimizing dependence on the motor car and supporting public
transport. Crowded roads mean more animals killed directly
(especially if we go too fast), loss of habitat to *more* roads and
more creatures poisoned by fumes, including ourselves!

CHAPTER SEVEN

Living Without Cruelty

By now it will be clear that 'living without cruelty' does not mean being kind to animals at the expense of humans. On the contrary, the two are inseparable. In this chapter I will try to look at vegetarianism in its widest context and will suggest just a few of the ways in which the challenge which a non-meat diet represents is intrinsically related to other issues relating to food production.

FOOD SUPPLY AND THE THIRD WORLD

To begin with, we will return to the issue of food supply and developing nations. As we have seen, increasing areas of land have been turned over to growing feed, either for newly developed factory farms in the country of origin or for export to factory farms in the West. Another example of this can be found in India, which multiplied its production of soya by five times between 1974 and 1982, almost all of the crop finding its way into the stomachs of livestock raised in rich nations rather than into hungry mouths.[1] The point is, however, that it is not only animal feed which is wasting valuable land. When grown on a massive scale, tea, coffee, cocoa, cotton and sugar, for example, come into the same category of cash crops which diminish the areas available for feeding humans. In all, Oxfam estimates that 'more than one-quarter of the land on which crops are grown in the Third World today is given over to non-food crops'.[1]

A vicious circle has been created. Governments in Third

World countries depend upon foreign exchange to meet debts, and therefore manipulate their own markets to ensure that it becomes advantageous for farmers to grow crops for export. Alas, the money received for these exports does not really help, because as a result of land being turned over to non-food produce there is not enough food grown to feed their own population. Consequently, money has then to be spent on importing grain to feed the hungry. This problem is increasing. In 1960, the Third World as a whole imported 20 million tonnes of grain; now the figure has risen to 100 million tonnes.[1] Manipulation of prices by powerful Western governments has resulted in poor nations often paying increased prices for grain imports, while prices for their exports fall. As a result, we find the Third World becoming deeper and deeper in debt to the West and their people with ever-diminishing areas left to grow their own traditional food crops. Ultimately, this may leave the poorer people without sufficient money to farm their own land and they may then be forced to leave their homes.

In other words, the contribution of the meat and particularly the poultry industries is only one important part of an unfair world economic system, based upon the West manipulating the Third World in order to seek its own benefits. Rather than helping the poorer countries to improve and develop their traditional agriculture (the majority of which is vegetarian), we interfere to suit our own requirements for luxury. Therefore, if you are concerned about the wasted resources involved in meat production, you should. logically, also be outraged by other injustices which are practised upon developing nations. It may seem a long way away, but small practical measures can be taken. If we are not willing to boycott our luxuries completely, we may at least wish to pay a little more for products like tea and coffee purchased from organizations like Oxfam and the World Development Movement in the knowledge that a guaranteed fair price has been paid to the workers who produced them.

DISCRIMINATION

As we know well, agricultural systems in other nations exploit human labour on the grounds of colour of skin, religion, political sympathies, caste or even sex. It would be irrational of anybody opposed to the oppression of animals in food production to support racism or apartheid in any of its ugly manifestations. If we care for the sort of values which vegetarianism promotes, we should support unequivocally any pressure that can be brought against nations or political parties which discriminate against or imprison and torture other humans on such grounds. In a more rational and stable world this would hardly need saying, yet already in the UK we have some concerted efforts by neo-fascist organizations to infiltrate animal-rights groups, claiming to support their aims.

FOOD PRODUCTION, CHEMICAL STYLE

If we now leave the Third World and move to our own half of the planet, we see a different kind of problem. Here we are not lacking in food or scientific development. On the contrary, it is precisely these factors which threaten the health of humans and are responsible for a system of food production chillingly violent to animals. Apart from factory farming and slaughter, this is also evident in the increasing use of fertilizers, pesticides, herbicides and insecticides and in the addition of chemical additives to preserve, stabilize, colour or flavour our food. As with the intensification of the livestock industry, widespread application of these substances has little to do with feeding people adequately. Rather, the prime motive is normally profit. Just as animals are manipulated in order to obtain as much flesh as possible by the cheapest method available, so more and more nitrogen fertilizers are applied to food crops for the financial benefits of the agrochemical industry, even though massive food surpluses exist throughout the EEC and higher yields are the last thing we need. Similarly, farming is becoming increasingly dependent upon chemicals to control pests, with the seeming effect that more serious pest problems are developing, requiring yet more chemicals. Food manufacturers also add chemical additives routinely to finished products, largely because flavourings, colourings and artificial preservatives are cheaper than natural substances.

SPREADING THE CHEMICALS FAR AND WIDE

The frightening acceleration in the application of chemicals to grow food has created immeasurable health risks. Until 50 years ago the human diet was uncontaminated with such additives. Now it is extremely difficult to purchase crops that have not been treated with chemicals. By a process comparable to the way in which farm animals develop resistance to the drugs supposedly administered to destroy harmful bacteria, the target plant invariably gathers a resistance to chemical intervention. As a result, a crop that might have endured one spray 20 years ago may now receive several doses: four to six sprays per year is the average on non-organic farms in the UK.

We are assured by vested interests that these chemicals are perfectly safe. Are they? Since their only real purpose is to kill other things, it does seem the height of human arrogance to assume that we are totally immune, particularly when spraying methods are so inefficient. Surveys have shown that more than four-fifths of pesticide-carrying spray is released in droplets so small that they never settle on the target plant, but instead remain potent in the air. In time, the accumulation of these droplets results in humans breathing 'air whose poison overburden increases everytime the sprayers are used'.[2] A report by the Soil Association on this issue argues further that many pesticides 'are related to nerve gases banned from warfare' and that this 'major scandal' could explain 'so many of the diseases and deformities to which our population becomes prey'.[2] Even though the spray-drift part of the problem could at least be improved by more efficient equipment, the long-term dangers created to both wildlife and humans by our dependence on chemicals cannot be overestimated. *New Scientist* states that 'unchecked and widespread use' is 'slowly but surely killing some of Britain's wildlife',[3] while many commentators, dating back to Rachel Carson in *Silent Spring*,[4] have warned that 'not only the target insect or plant but anything—human or non-human— within range of the chemical fallout may know the sinister touch of the poison'. Evidence is growing that hundreds of people in Great Britain suffer sub-acute pesticide poisoning after being exposed to farm chemicals. Friends of the Earth have estimated that up to 60% of pesticide sprayed from aircraft drifts more than 305 metres from the target and this is cited as a cause of many reports of illness. Symptoms including flu-like ailments such as aching limbs, eye irritation, chest complaints, dizziness, disorientation and depression are reported commonly in areas where spraying has taken place.[5]

The movement for vegetarianism needs to embrace the case for organic farming, not simply because it will result in more healthy food for us all, but rather because the lack of concern for living creatures and the environment epitomized by the agrochemical industry is part of the same destructive spirit characterized by the meat industry. For it is an horrific fact that the 500 million animals slaughtered in our abattoirs annually probably represent only a small proportion of the total killed by pesticides and other chemicals which either poison directly or kill the food plants on which our wildlife depends for sustenance. Even if organic food is more expensive monetarily, vegetarians should support chemical-free produce wherever possible. Apart from using our purchasing power, we can also take effective political action by writing to supermarkets in the hope of making organic foods more readily available. Already, Safeways (UK), Sainsburys and selected superstores sell a limited range of fruit and vegetables. Likewise, those who possess their own gardens or allotments may sometimes be tempted to control persistent weeds with chemical treatment, but we must first ask whether in doing so, we bring ourselves into conflict with the spirit behind our meat-free diet? It has been estimated that 900 grams of chemicals are applied each year to every hectare of British gardens and there are more than 500 garden chemicals to choose from.

Any condemnation of chemically grown crops is certain to raise a smile amongst cynics. How, they may ask, can we claim that vegetarian food is more healthy than meat-eating when almost all of it is obtained by the liberal application of those substances we abhor? There is some truth in this argument. Vegetarians cannot ignore the fact that only by encouraging organic farming can we be sure to obtain the most healthy foods available. On the other hand, we are still better off than meat-eaters because chemical residues become more potent when we eat higher up the food chain. Chemicals taken by animals from their feed are stored in a more concentrated form. Rachel Carson estimated that 'an intake of as little one-tenth or 1 part per million in the diet results in a storage of about 10 to 15 parts per million, an increase of 1 hundred fold or more. In the diet of an average home, meat and any product derived from animal fats contain the heaviest residues of chlorinated hydrocarbons and other pesticides'.[4]

FOOD PROCESSING

Thus far, we have dealt with what we might call the raw products of food production. Inevitably, however, the same greed and misuse of scientific ingenuity is also apparent during the processing of our food. Like pesticides, chemical food additives are a relatively new phenomenon. Despite recent concern, their use has doubled over the last ten years and there are now approximately 3500 added to the food we eat. By 1984, the average consumer ate 2·5 kilograms of them per year.[6] They represent another example of our diet having become dependent upon ingredients whose long-term effects on our health are unknown. Already doubts have emerged about many substances, leading the Food Advisory Committee to admit that 'more evidence of safety is required'. Several doctors have also voiced disquiet, raising possible associations between additives and the spread of allergies, nervous disorders, cancer and arthritis. Moreover, many E numbers are derived either wholly or partly from animal products, e.g. colouring agents: E104, 120, 124, 132, 153; preservatives: E270, 280, 282; antioxidants: E304, 322, 325–7, 334; emulsifiers, stabilizers and thickeners: E405, 422, 454, 470–5, 477, 480–3.

THE ANIMAL CONNECTION

The possible implications for human health are an important reason for opposing the infiltration of the chemical industry into all areas of food production. Yet there is another important reason, which highlights once again our central thesis that human and other animal exploitation are inseparable. The deplorable truth is that almost all garden and agricultural chemicals and food additives (plus most household products and cosmetics) are assessed for safety by tests upon animals. These can include eye and skin irritancy, carcinogenicity, teratogenicity and toxicity tests to determine how poisonous a product might be. The latter normally involves dosing an animal either orally, by inserting a tube down the throat, or through injection. Eventually a figure of potential toxicity is reached by finding the amounts of a substance needed to kill a percentage of the creatures used. Animals may die in agony.

It would be another example of irrationality to be against the killing of animals for food and yet at the same time to support animal experimentation. To seek to benefit humans by inflicting pain and misery on other living creatures is surely unacceptable to all those who refuse to countenance bloodshed in the production of food? Many eminent figures have expressed condemnation of vivisection throughout the late nineteenth and twentieth century, none more succinctly than Mark Twain when he wrote:

> I believe I am not interested to know whether vivisection produces results that are profitable for the human race or doesn't. To know the results are profitable to the race would not remove my hostility to it. The pain which it inflicts upon unconsenting animals is the basis of my hostility towards it, and it is to me sufficient justification of the enmity without looking further.[7]

Yet alas, despite the opposition of Mark Twain and others, the use of animals continues to be the accepted method of researching new products, medical or otherwise. In other words, despite the fact that we now know how closely animals resemble humans in their abilities to feel and even to think, their enslavement and torture is still considered morally acceptable.

One recent experiment which highlights our failure to confront the ethical problem took place in the USA, where a female chimpanzee was made pregnant using male human sperm. Although the half-human, half-ape creature was aborted, 'because of the moral, social and ethical questions involved' the basis of the experiment was that 'chimpanzees are very similar to humans'. One of those who took part, Italian anthropologist Brunetto Chiarelli, then added that 'the purpose of such a subhuman creature would be in the use of doing monotonous routines or dirty jobs'.[8] As extreme as this Frankensteinish example appears, it actually focuses perfectly the illogicality of all animal experiments. On the one hand, the justification offered is that the animal is 'very similar to humans' and on the other, the animal produced remains 'subhuman', excluded from all moral protection. Surely, if animals are 'very similar to humans' they should be entitled to the same protection from abuse. If they are not like us then there seems little point in carrying out the experiments.

The question which no supporter of vivisection ever has (or ever will) manage to answer satisfactorily is this: Exactly what are the qualities animals lack which entitles us to, for example, blind, burn, irradiate or poison them in laboratories? We now know scientifically as well as instinctively, that it is not intelligence, it is not reason and it is not feeling.

The truth is that while animals have the capacity to feel, think, experience joy, pain and sorrow and form close bonds with others of the same species or a close maternal bond, their qualities and the ways in which they express these are different from humans.

For this reason, if we do want to look further than the moral question, we find that the scientific validity of animal experiments is anyway highly questionable. In an investigation of possible health hazards associated with food additives, for example, *New Scientist* found that research on animals (the only safety test conducted) was 39% accurate. The conclusion drawn was that you could gain more appropriate evidence by tossing a coin![9] The World Health Organisation has estimated that humans are ten times more sensitive to additives than animals. 'To determine a safe level of use for man, a dose which has an effect in animals is divided by 100—which makes assumptions about the action of toxic substances which could be widely inaccurate.'[10]

THE CHAIN OF SUFFERING:
ANIMALS – THE THIRD WORLD – CONSUMERS

It is evident that within our food and agricultural industries, there are forces whose concern for profit far overrides their interest in life. The scientific invalidity of animal experimentation, let alone the barbarism, is only one aspect of a totally callous indifference at work. Consumers in our own society are often themselves victims in a chain in which the animal butchered in the laboratory or slaughterhouse always seems to be the first and most defenceless casualty. The poor in the Third World can also suffer in the same chain of indifference. For instance, pesticides, which include active ingredients such as Disulotin, Terbasos and NOC, whose use is either banned or severely restricted in Great Britain or other industrialized nations, are exported to the Third World, often without labels to explain potential dangers. Three-quarters of the world's pesticides fatalities are in developing nations, even though they use only a small percentage of the total output worldwide. Oxfam has estimated that 375 000 people in poorer countries are poisoned by pesticides every year, 100 000 of them fatally.[11] Remember that these figures do not even include chronic or long-term damage, such as cancers, birth defects or sterility. The explanation for these deplorable statistics is that as government controls become stricter in industrialized nations, more and more countries look to the poor half of the world, where legislation is more lax, to dump their unsafe products. In 1975, 25% of pesticides exported to the Third World by the USA were either banned or unregistered in the country of origin. In Great Britain, where such information is kept secret, it is known that more than one-quarter of the income of the British pesticide industry is obtained from exports.

Against all this insanity, vegetarianism stands for a concern for all life. Just as the profits made from agrobusiness, as a result of animal suffering in factory farms and slaughterhouses, cannot be seen in isolation from the issues of world hunger or the diseases of affluence among our own populations, so profits made by the agrochemical industry are based: (a) upon exploitation of animals for research; (b) upon exploitation of the poor in developing nations to whom doubtful substances are sold; and (c) upon exploitation of the human population in the Western World, where the long-term effects of chemicals remain unknown. All the evidence shows that the ruthlessness of the meat industry has its parallel in other areas of food production.

CHAPTER EIGHT

Vivisection

Many people will resist my diagnosis of the food, agro-chemical and meat industries. After all, it will be argued, there is now more food in the Western World than ever before: few people go hungry, productivity has increased enormously and an expanding range of foodstuffs are available. Surely these are signs of success not failure?

The answer is, of course, that while all these develop-ments are undeniable, we have basically exchanged the evil of ill health due to poverty for another form of malnu-trition, namely, illness created by too many unhealthy products. While social, economic and scientific advances have produced the capacity to ensure that everybody could now receive both an adequate and a healthy diet, the commercial interests responsible have largely squandered the opportunity in the interests of their own profits. Indis-putably the profit motive is responsible for a considerable proportion of the preventable diseases which ruin our health in the Western World. The most obvious example is the way in which tobacco companies continue to advertise widely, despite the proven evil of their products. They are allowed to do so largely because the Treasury receives £4000 million every year from tobacco tax[1] and this over-rides the fact that the cost to the NHS of tobacco-induced illness runs into millions of pounds each year. Likewise, a combination of Parliamentary influence and money created for the Treasury allows the food, agrochemical, alcohol and pharmaceutical lobbies (to name only four) to wreck the nation's health without strong official condemnation. In this chapter, we will look a little closer at one of those vested interests—the pharmaceutical industry.

Although at first glance this may seem a long way divorced from our central subject of vegetarianism, closer examination will reveal that the parallels between drug and food production are both too obvious and too disturbing to overlook. The association between them is particularly disturbing because these are two areas of life where commercial interest should be governed by the purist principles of benefitting public health. Yet the fact is that they are two of our major sources of illness. Is it pure coincidence that both are also centred to a great extent upon animal suffering? I think not. Food production in the Western World is based upon the slaughterhouse, while our medical system revolves largely around the vivisection laboratory. Almost two million animals are used yearly in drug research in the UK alone and the majority of the public accept this as necessary. After all, are not the drug companies producing new pharmaceuticals to conquer disease? The facts present rather a different picture. There are 18 000 medicaments, containing 3000 drug formulas on the British market alone. How many of these are necessary? Perhaps the best indication comes from the World Health Organisation, which established that only approximately 200 known drugs are important for the treatment of existing major illness in the Third World.[2] If this is the case, it is surely unthinkable that we should need any more drugs for treatment in the 'healthier' developed nations? Confirming this proposition, researchers at Newcastle University found that 143 drugs would meet 90% of the prescriptions which GPs have to issue.[3]

Many of the new drugs brought onto the market are unnecessary 'me-too' variations on already existing formulae, offering similar treatment in an area already over-prescribed. Worse still, treatments are often motivated more by the need to create secondary prescriptions, rather than a desire to cure illness. To give an example, the most commonly prescribed substances in the UK are tranquillizers, sedatives and sleeping pills. Of approximately one million patients who take them, an estimated 10% (100 000) suffer symptoms of addiction.[4] Benzodiazines (e.g. Mogadon, Valium and Librium) are mainly responsible, often causing distressing and prolonged withdrawal problems. Yet rather than looking for a reduction in the availability of such substances (which anyway usually only suppress deep-rooted unhappiness) the Medical Research Council has instead offered grants to discover a drug which will alleviate withdrawal symptoms created by the original prescription![5]

Sometimes the side-effects of drugs are far worse than withdrawal problems. Several drugs have been taken off the market in recent years, declared unsafe after causing human death, in spite of numerous tests on animals having supposedly indicated otherwise. In all, an estimated 7000 deaths annually in the UK are associated with NHS prescriptions[6] with between 5% and 18% of hospital beds occupied by people suffering from drug side-effects[7]. According to the pharmaceutical companies' own figures, 40% of drugs on the market have been developed in the last 20 years.[8] Yet how many of these have brought important medical advances? Dr Donald Gould, author of *The Medical Mafia*, puts it succinctly: 'No more than a handful have made any dramatic contribution to the welfare of the sick and probably a larger number have had a tragically opposite effect'.[8]

THE CHAIN OF SUFFERING AGAIN

From a vegetarian viewpoint, there are several important questions raised by this level of waste and corruption within pharmaceutical research. Is a health system which exists upon what one defender of animal experiments, Peter Ronner, himself labelled 'the living nightmare of vivisection'[9] inevitably limited in its capacity to provide the most fitting care for human patients? Is there not a terrible contradiction in the concept of pursuing medical knowledge to benefit humans by inflicting pain on defence-less creatures imprisoned against their will? To raise such reservations is not to deny that there are many caring individuals working within our modern medical system, nor that there are occasions when drug treatments are necessary and beneficial to humanity. Yet at the same time the corruption at the centre of the pharmaceutical industry is undeniable, creating three categories of victims:

1 Laboratory animals, inflicted with hideous diseases in order to test products upon them.
2 The human beings least able to defend themselves in Third world nations, where drugs either banned or proven ineffective in the West are marketed because the same restrictions on sales do not exist. Perhaps the most shameful example has been the promotion of anabolic steroids offered as a treatment for malnutrition, even though the companies involved knew that they were ineffective, stunted bone growth, caused irreversible masculinization of girls and frequently led to tumours of the liver.[10] Less spectacularly, dishonest advertising is ripe. In Brazil, for example, 'two-thirds of the remedies on sale don't have the effect they say, don't have any scientific basis'.[11] Drugs with potentially fatal side-effects are promoted for minor complaints, often sold over the counter with the help of glossy advertising. It is all too common for the poor to be manipulated into wasting money they can ill afford on vitamins, tonics or more dangerous substances. Of the £1000 million income which Great Britain receives from drug exports (no wonder governments do not intervene!) over one third comes from Third World nations.[10]
3 Our own population are also victims, as illustrated by the epidemic in drug-induced illness and the dishonest advertising methods employed. Approximately £5000 per annum is spent by drug firms on every GP in the

UK.[3] Standard promotional procedures include making false claims about the potential of substances to cure disease, suppression of information on side-effects and the offer of personal incentives to encourage doctors to prescribe new products. The rise in drug prescriptions by 25% over a ten-year period in the 1970s has little to do with the discovery of effective new treatments; rather, as the World Health Organisation states, 'promotional activities of the manufacturers have created a demand greater than the actual needs'.[12]

FIGHTING VIVISECTION IN THE KITCHEN

To prove that there is a profound connection between animal and human abuse does not mean that if we could rid our food production of slaughterhouses and our medical system of vivisection laboratories we would automatically cure all our ills. Such a claim would be extraordinarily naive. What we can claim justifiably, however, is that exploitation of *non-human* life is at the very least a central feature in some of the worst examples of preventable misery being inflicted upon *humans* in the world today. Consequently, for individuals to free themselves as far as possible from products which involve animal suffering is more than a gesture to the suffering of other living creatures. Ultimately, their pain is our pain too. Indeed, it could be argued that to turn vegetarian seems a particularly significant step to take in opposition to all this misery, since no other action so aptly embraces the concepts of compassion for all creatures, rational use of resources and a healthy diet for all.

Moreover, to link vegetarianism even further with the vivisection issue, it is probably one of the most useful steps we can take to undermine drug-company claims for more animal research. Given the health advantages associated with a non-animal diet and the fact that we live in an age where every human ailment will be seen as another excuse to inflict experiments upon animals, it is almost our duty to do everything within our powers to maintain good health. Being careful about what you eat may seem an insignificant gesture, but it is undeniable that nutrition and other environmental considerations have played a far bigger part in conquering killer diseases in the past than medical intervention. The deadly nineteenth-century epidemics of infectious diseases, e.g. scarlet fever, TB, bronchitis,pneumonia,influenza, whooping cough,measles, diphtheria and smallpox, plus the food- and water-borne infections, such as cholera, typhoid and diarrhoea, 'were declining before and in most cases long before specific therapy became available'.[13] They were conquered largely by rising standards of living, particularly improved hygiene, water and housing conditions. In the words of Pasteur's biographer, Rene Dubos, 'by the time laboratory medicine came effectively into the picture the job had been carried far toward completion by the humanitarian and social reformers of the nineteenth century'.[14] Similarly, infant mortality had fallen from 150 to 50 babies per thousand dying prior to their first birthday *before* the therapeutic revolution had begun, so the assumption must be that 'the major force for change has been a better standard of living—better housing, better nutrition, better conditions at work'.[15] It was primarily poverty and lack of hygiene that killed people, not lack of drugs, just as it is today in the Third World. In the developing nations it is precisely the same illnesses which killed people on a large scale in the West a hundred years ago that are the main causes of mortality. For instance, 3·5 million children die each year from measles, TB, polio, whooping cough, diptheria and tetanus and no amount of Western medicine, however useful in certain circumstances, will ever solve the problem of high infant mortality before nutrition and environmental hygiene are improved significantly.[16]

In the West cancer and heart disease are our twentieth-century equivalents of the nineteenth-century diseases of poverty. Instead of being created by lack of food and clean water, they are a direct result of our technological age. It is ludicrous that millions of animals bred in sterile conditions are sacrificed each year in a bid to find modern-day cures, when both history and common sense tell us that large reductions in death rates are not likely to be brought about by medicines developed through vivisection. Taking cancer as a specific example, increasing numbers of people are beginning to accept that animal research is largely irrelevant. *The Lancet* has stated that 'no animal tumour is closely related to cancer in humans'[17] and in the *British Medical Journal* we read that 'whilst studies were starting, warning voices were suggesting that data from research on animals could not be used to develop a treatment for human tumours'.[18]

These kinds of reservations are being expressed about other areas of animal research too. In the words of Professor Dollery of Hammersmith Hospital: 'For the great majority of disease entities, the animal models either do not exist or are really very poor',[19] whilst in the *New Scientist* E. Lesser writes that 'no amount of animal experimentation can ensure the safety of drugs for human beings'.[20] Indeed, the different ways in which different species react to drugs should have alerted us to the need for a more humane medical system many years ago: morphine sedates people and rats, yet excites cats and mice; aspirin causes birth defects in rats, mice, guinea-pigs, cats, dogs and monkeys but not in pregnant women; chloroform anaesthetizes humans but kills dogs; penicillin is poisonous to guinea-pigs.[21]

PUTTING IT IN PERSPECTIVE

To end this chapter by restating reservations I put forward in Chapter 2: there is no guarantee that a well-balanced vegetarian diet will save any individual from cancer, heart disease or any other suffering. Nor could it be argued that animal experiments have taught human beings nothing. Animals have been sacrificed in their billions and it would be defying all laws of probability to say that nowhere did any of this modern-day blood sacrifice result in some knowledge that did not serve medical treatment in humans. The truth is, however, that the value of animal experimentation has been very much overestimated. (For a detailed analysis of the waste of animal life in medical research see *The Cruel Deception* by Dr Robert Sharpe.[22]) In the meantime, until the day of abolition arrives, it remains more imperative than ever before that those concerned about animal cruelty remember the maxim 'we are what we eat'. Through a humane and healthy diet, we can at least point the way towards an ethical health system.

CHAPTER NINE

Beyond the Food Cupboard

To promote vegetarianism, or more radically still the concept that we should try to live our lives without products that cause any deliberate suffering to animals, is to invite all kinds of hostility. In particular, we are accused of inflicting cranky views upon others or of attempting to impinge upon freedom of choice. Frequently we hear the meat industry argue that while they have no objection to vegetarianism in principle, what they cannot tolerate is any attempt to convert people away from meat diets. The irony of all this is that whilst the voice of the vegetarian population represents nothing more than a vociferous minority, insignificant in terms of finance, the meat industry and others with a vested interest in animal suffering spend comparative fortunes attempting to dictate public taste. In 1987 alone, the Meat and Livestock Commission raised a budget of £13·68 million to stimulate sales:[1] this money is spent solely on advertising meat as a product and represents only a small proportion of advertising by individual meat companies promoting particular products. The story is the same for other products involving animal exploitation. Over-the-counter medicines and household goods of all descriptions, ranging from oven cleaners to fresh-air sprays and cough mixtures are all metaphorically pushed down the public's throat in an attempt to make profits. Almost all of them involve a wide range of animal suffering in their production and, equally, almost all of them are unnecessary to human existence.

In this chapter, we shall once again look at 'living

without cruelty' in its widest context and show that to embrace the idea we have to educate ourselves to resist a barrage of propaganda and sales promotion which is thrust upon us daily. Only by doing so will we be able to see how 'living without cruelty' can become a more practical alternative than we might otherwise assume.

COSMETICS

Cosmetics tested on animals are among the easiest commodities to avoid. In almost every case they are simply unnecessary and on no grounds can they possibly justify the blinding and poisoning of other living creatures. Although the number of animals used has declined in recent years, experiments are still undertaken, such as force-feeding the human equivalent of 1·8 kilograms of lipstick formulations in toxicity tests.[2] Luckily, it is not simply a choice between experiments or no cosmetics: nothing could be further from the truth. A growing number of companies now produce goods ranging from perfumes to shampoos, oils, skin creams and lotions, soaps, make-up, sun-tan lotions and haircare products without sinking to the disgrace of animal tests. Ingredients known to be safe and gentle are employed and human volunteers do the testing.

Another alternative is to make your own cosmetics. By growing, harvesting and preserving herbs it is possible to take full care of the hair, skin and body. For those who wish to pursue this idea further, Camilla Hepper's book, *Herbal Cosmetics*[3] is strongly recommended. When you do buy cosmetics be sure to avoid hidden animal products. Slaughterhouse by-products frequently used include tallow, stearic acid and glycerine. Civet (the sex glands of civet cats) and musk (musk pods from male deer) are sometimes utilized as part of the scent or fixative.

HOUSEHOLD GOODS

The public does not normally associate the numerous household products which appear on the retail market with animal experiments, yet each 'new', 'improved' or 'advanced' washing powder, carpet cleaner, air freshener and toilet cleaner, to name but a few products, will most likely have been developed by using animals in the following range of tests. The same tests (specifically those for eye and skin irritancy and toxicity) are also routinely carried out by cosmetic companies.

The Draize eye-irritancy test

The test substances are applied to the eyes of conscious rabbits. They can be left for up to seven days to determine whether the condition of the eye improves or deteriorates over a period of time after contact with the chemicals. No pain relief is given and symptoms may include redness, swelling, haemorrhage, ulceration and discharge.

The Draize skin test

Fur is shaved from the animals' back and the skin abraded. The test substance is then applied and covered. Symptoms may include inflammation, swelling and tissue damage.

Toxicity testing

Animals are dosed with different amounts of the test substance to discover the doses which will kill half of them (LD50). In the classic test, between 30 and 100 animals are used to test each substance. No pain relief is given and animals could be left for up to 14 days in severe pain before death intervenes. The classic LD50 test is no longer required by law, being increasingly replaced by the limit test which uses fewer animals. Long-term toxicity tests are also undertaken using lower levels of the substance over a period of months.

Carcinogenicity

In an attempt to discover the possible cancer risk of a new chemical, animals may be dosed for months or even years to see whether tumours develop.

Teratogenicity

Since the Thalidomide tragedy, when damage was caused to the embryos of pregnant mothers, chemicals are now tested for teratogenicity. Pregnant animals (usually rats and rabbits, occasionally monkeys) are exposed to the substance, mainly by mouth or injection, and shortly before birth the young are delivered by Caesarean section, so that the womb can be examined for any young that may have died during pregnancy. The young are studied for obvious abnormalities and are killed and sectioned for microscopic investigation. Ten to twenty animals are treated in this way during each test.

Apart from the moral objections to these tests, it is also worth pointing out that they are all very limited and often misleading scientifically, despite the fact that they are supposedly undertaken in order to establish human safety. The rabbit's eye, for instance, is physiologically different to the human eye and, therefore, as one group of industrial researchers has concluded, 'it has not been possible for us to use the results of rabbit studies to predict accurately the actual irritation that might occur in humans after accidental exposure'.[4] As far as toxicology tests are concerned, the British Petroleum toxicologist Dr Sharatt has stated that 'as an index of acute toxicity, this (LD50 Test) is valueless'.[5] Research for carcinogens in animals is also fraught with grave shortcomings because humans and the favourite research animals, rats and mice, react differently and suffer from different kinds of cancers. For instance, 'compounds that cause hepatomas (liver cancers) in mice may not always be carcinogenic in rats, or if carcinogenic in both species may have different target sites. The extrapolation of such results to define any risk to humans remains a troublesome problem'.[6] Scientists are also usually prepared to admit that testing teratogens in animals has little predictive power for effects in people. Dr P. Lewis of the Department of Clinical Pharmacology the Royal Post-graduate Medical School of London has written that:

> ... unfortunately species variation in the sensitivity to drug teratogenicity is very widespread. Even within a species considerable variation can be demonstrated between different animal strains ... faced with such complexity it is not surprising that teratological testing based on animal tests has a poor predictive power and is thought to do little more than exclude grossly toxic substances. As yet there is no indication as to how this stalemate may be broken.[7]

Despite such evidence, the battery of animal tests goes on and on. For what reason? Looking at the supermarket shelves nowadays it is hard to believe that human beings have survived adequately for thousands of years without 'special action' or 'all-in-one' toilet cleaners. Indeed, toilets seem a particular area of fascination! Traditionally, soda crystals and hot water did the job. Then we had the first 'all-in-one' lavatory cleaners. After several 'improvements' on these, industrial researchers came up with lavatory cleaners which include deodorants. Now we have gone one step further and have not only deodorants but also colourants. What next we may ask!

ALTERNATIVE HOUSEHOLD PRODUCTS

The alternatives do exist and prove the point that strength and conviction to resist marketing and advertising is something that vegetarians must learn to master early.

Here are some general rules:

1 Avoid buying anything labelled 'new', 'advanced' or 'improved'. It almost certainly means more animals will hae been sacrificed in search of the improvements.

2 One company recommended is Ecover. Many health- or wholefood shops now sell their range of products, including washing powder, cream cleanser, toilet cleaner, fabric conditioner, wool-wash liquid, floor soap, heavy-duty hand-cleaner and washing-up liquid. Currently, some of these do include whey, but I understand the company is hoping to replace the whey with soya products, thus making the whole range suitable for vegans. Although the cost of Ecover products may at first sight appear high, they can be used sparingly and do last a long time, and they have the particular advantage of being biodegradable, i.e. they include no chemical ingredients potentially harmful to the environment. The company also guarantees that they are not tested upon animals.

Faith Products' Clear Spring liquid washing powder is another ecological, non-animal-based product warmly recommended, as are the limited range of goods made by the Caurnie Soap Company.

3 Some supermarkets do sell some household products which they claim have not been tested on animals. These include International's washing-up liquid, washing powder and floor and wall cleaners; Safeway's washing-up liquid and Spar's blue washing powder, automatic washing powder and washing-up liquid. Acdo washing powder is also supposed to be cruelty-free.

4 Finally, there are a whole host of 'traditional' cleaning methods. Before mass marketing, humans relied on certain basic ingredients, such as bleach, vinegar and washing soda. Although it is probable that these substances will have been tested on animals at some time, research is likely to have taken place many years ago. Table 9·1 will give you a few ideas but literally hundreds of similar 'granny' recipes exist.

Table 9·1 Do-it-yourself cruelty-free household products

Purpose or problem	Method
All-purpose cleaner	1 Bleach 2 3 tbsp baking soda and 1 qrt water made into paste
Sinks and ovens	Soda crystals in hot water
Microwave ovens	3 tbsp baking soda and 1 litre water made into paste. For persistent odours leave open box of baking soda inside, removing before each use
Furniture cleaner	1 Mix 1 tsp turpentine, 3 tbsp linseed oil and 1 litre hot water. Stir well and allow to cool. Use on cloth 2 3 parts olive oil to 1 part vinegar applied with soft cloth 3 1 part lemon juice with 2 parts olive oil applied with soft cloth
Window cleaner	Plain water with dash of vinegar
General stains	1 1 tsp white vinegar to 3 tsp warm water. Leave to dry and apply a little detergent, dry again and vacuum 2 Eucalyptus oil
Oil stains	White chalk rubbed in before washing
Linoleum floor cleaner/wax	Mop with 1 cup white vinegar mixed with 9 litres water to remove greasy film
Grease marks on wallpaper	Make thick paste from cleaning fluid and french

Table 9·1 (*Continued*)

Purpose or problem	Method
	chalk. Apply to spot, leave overnight and then brush off carefully
Toilet bowl	Vinegar or ammonia
Mildew remover	Lemon juice or white vinegar and salt
Saucepan cleaner	Soak in baking-soda solution before washing
Air freshener	1 Incense 2 Pot pourri (mixture of dried herbs and oils) 3 Open box of baking soda
Fruit, grass and biro stains	Methylated spirits
Loosening dirt and restoring whiteness to clothes	Ammonia
Water softener	Washing soda or one-quarter cup white vinegar
Brass cleaner	Salt
Copper cleaner	Paste of lemon juice, salt and flour
Blocked pipes	1 Bicarbonate of soda 2 1–2 cups baking soda followed by one-half cup vinegar
Car headlights, mirror and windscreen	Wipe with damp cloth or sponge sprinkled with dry baking soda. Rinse with water and dry with soft towel

Table 9·1 (*Continued*)

Purpose or problem	Method
Ant repellent	1 Vinegar and water. Wash countertops, cabinets and floors 2 A line of tartar across the area where the ants are entering
Pet 'accidents'	Alcohol or ammonia and hot water
Flea and tick repellents	Feed animal brewer's yeast and garlic. Fennel, rue and rosemary repel fleas

OVER-THE-COUNTER MEDICINES

Medicines can be put into two categories: those that can be obtained without a prescription from chemists and those that can be purchased after the approval of a medical practitioner. The former are normally for minor complaints and include pain-killers, eye drops, digestion tablets and powders, cough mixtures and cold cures. Yet again these drugs will have involved the normal routine animal tests. In addition, many of them are both useless and hazardous.

Britain spends more than £40 million per year on cough remedies yet an investigation by the *Drugs and Therapeutics Bulletin* has stated that many of them contain ingredients which have the opposite effects, i.e. cough suppressants and cough stimulants in the same bottle. Dr Collier, Senior Lecturer in Clinical Pharmacology at St. Georges Hospital, comments that it is 'ludicrous to take mixtures that contain one ingredient to make you cough and another to take it away'.[8] Cough medicines appear to be a hotchpotch of potential health problems. The *British National Formulary* (the doctor's standard guide to medi-

cines), has concluded that there is 'lack of evidence that
the ingredients have any effect'.[9] The advice of doctors is
that 'if a cough suppressant is not considered clinically
necessary the patient should be warned against buying one
over the counter': some that claim to soothe dry, irritating
coughs contain glycerol which can damage teeth and
others may be addictive.

ALTERNATIVES TO OVER-THE-COUNTER MEDICINES

Whatever treatment you try, there is no drug or remedy
which can necessarily cure the common cold: Olbas Oil
(available from health-food shops) helps breathing and
clears the head; breathing in steam from a basin of very
hot water helps loosen catarrh; sucking a boiled sweet
sometimes helps tickly coughs, as can lemon and honey
in hot water. Some people also believe that a gram of
vitamin C a day relieves symptoms. Pertinently, as with
other problems, diet may also play its part. The nature-
cure approach is to cut out all dairy products, cakes and
biscuits, all of which tend to form mucus, and to increase
the intake of fresh fruits and raw vegetables.

Even when over-the-counter medicines are more effective, there is the additional problem of drug side-effects,
e.g. Phenacetin, a pain-killer included in over 80
compounds and marketed throughout this century, has
recently been banned after causing kidney and bladder
disease. Even aspirin is said to be responsible for 7000
hospital admissions each year in Great Britain alone
because of problems with stomach and intestinal bleeding
leading to anaemia. The pain-killer has also been linked
with the potentially lethal children's disease, Reyes
Syndrome, leading to all preparations for children under
12 containing the drug being withdrawn in June 1986.

It has to be remembered that all drugs cause some side-
effects and should always be avoided if possible. Moreover, the marketing techniques involved in the over-the-

counter medicine industry are every bit as cut-throat as those used for any other products. All drug companies want people to take as many medicines as possible and one of their ways of stimulating sales is by turning relatively minor complaints like migraine, constipation and indigestion (usually problems caused by life-style and diet) into diseases requiring medical treatment. It pays the drug industry for people to seek cures rather than to look at the actual cause of their complaints. If you do feel in need of treatment for these 'minor' ailments (some of which although 'minor' in medical terms can admittedly cause great pain and discomfort), you may first be interested in trying alternative medicines that are available over the counter. These almost certainly will not have been tested on animals.

Most health-food shops and some chemists sell biochemic remedies—small doses of the mineral salts found naturally in the body. These are available for almost every ailment, ranging from headaches, toothaches and period pains to hay fever. Although they do not work for everybody (indeed no medicine does), many people swear to their effectiveness. Biochemic tissues are completely harmless. Homeopathic and herbal remedies are also found in most health-food shops. Although a few scientists have done animal tests on some of the former, it can be stated categorically that most products have not been tested on animals. Indeed, homoeopathy was developed in the eighteenth century by tests on humans and this is still the normal method of research.

COMPLEMENTARY MEDICINE

For more serious illness, orthodox medicine may seem more tempting and, indeed, sometimes may be the answer. Yet again, however, it is not the only possibility and in some cases can prove positively injurious. At least as many people die from drug side-effects as in car accidents. In addition, there is a growing realization that frequent reliance upon drugs, particularly commonly prescribed substances like antibiotics, lowers resistance and leaves the body susceptible to infection. Although it would be misleading to depreciate all conventional medicines, those concerned about either animal abuse or their own health should ask themselves several questions before seeking orthodox help. First, given time and rest, will the symptoms cure themselves? Many diseases are self-limiting. Second, could the symptoms have a preventable cause? Could it be something included or lacking in my diet? Have I been subjecting myself to too much stress at work or in personal life and could some of this be avoided? Have I been in contact with agrochemicals, industrial waste, food additives or other pollutants that I can avoid? If, after answering all these questions, you still feel in need of medical treatment, would you consider trying an alternative form of medicine? Although many people feel that alternative medicine is 'cranky', the difference between orthodox and unorthodox is largely a question of professional organization and scientific theory.

Orthodox medicine, with the backing of the NHS and Acts of Parliament, works on the theory that patients receive treatment contrary to the symptoms from which they are suffering. Thus, cancer is treated by the destruction of cells and a fever by a drug which lowers temperatures. On the other hand, homoeopathy works by prescribing minute dosages of substances which produce the same effect as the symptoms. The theory is that these will stir the body's natural defence mechanisms into defeating the disease. Homoeopathic substances are normally obtained from herbs and minerals and this form of treatment is the only alternative method accepted by the NHS. Herbalism also works on the principle that certain substances will reinforce the body's ability to fight disease. Like homoeopathic practitioners, herbalists will not necessarily prescribe the same remedy for every individual. Personality and overall health are also taken into account. Chiropractic and osteopathy developed from the practice of bone-setting. Advocates argue that the manipulation of the spine and joints can be helpful in overcoming many illnesses, with the spine seen as the important centre of health and physical condition.

Naturopathy revolves primarily around the concept of proper diet. Natural food (almost always purely vegetarian) and pure water, combined sometimes with herbal, homoeopathic and biochemical treatments are recommended, as is counselling assistance to help reduce stress. The theory is that if we eat correctly, think clearly and follow a life-style in tune with the needs of our bodies then disease can usually either be avoided or overcome.

Other available alternative therapies include acupuncture, reflexology, aromatherapy and colour therapy. At present, they may sound weird or cranky, but as Prince Charles said in an often-quoted remark 'What is taken for today's unorthodoxy is probably going to be tomorrow's convention'.

CLOTHING

As if to prove the immense chasm between the 'living without cruelty' ideal and our current ethos, the subjects we have discussed by no means exhaust all areas of animal exploitation. Take clothing. Fur, leather, suede and wool all depend upon the use of animals, though obviously some products involve more suffering than others. The production of furs results in the death of more than 300 million animals world-wide annually. Each year 100 000 foxes are trapped in Great Britain alone. Somewhere or other, the coats of almost every species are seen as a source of profit. It seems barely credible that despite all the publicity highlighting the fate of wild animals trapped in snares and steel-tooth traps, the number of animals killed for the fur industry is increasing. This is particularly true of factory-farmed furs, with the number of arctic foxes, minks and rabbits bred in cages to feed the vanity market rising annually, even in the UK. There are now more than

40 million mink in this country's factory-fur farms.[10] It is true that most leather and suede goods are the by-products of the slaughterhouse rather than the direct cause of animal deaths. Mass slaughter of animals for the meat trade means a surplus of cheap leather and suede for the clothing industry. Fortunately, as depressing as it is to see so many animal coats as popular as ever, alternatives are easy to obtain. More difficult to avoid are cruelty-free shoes, bags and wallets, though there is now a growing market for man-made fabrics—canvas, nylon and plastic—plus cotton goods. These are improving in quality all the time and can be found easily with a little effort. Even synthetic walking boots are now on the market (Westsports, 17 Fleet Street, Swindon, Wiltshire).

Man-made fabrics, such as acrylic, together with cotton goods, have also become a popular substitute for wool in clothing. While replacing woollen goods is unlikely to prove a first priority for vegetarians, it is another area where exploitation of animals is inevitable. Genetic breeding has resulted in less-hardy and well-adapted animals, manipulated to produce higher quality and bigger fleeces. Some of these breeds are unsuited to the harsh climates in which they are sometimes reared. Genetic breeding has also resulted in deformities such as leg weakness and the need for mutilations like tail docking. Moreover, like all other farm animals, sheep bred commercially end their life in the slaughterhouse long before their natural life is over, going first through all the traumas of transportation. A further problem is that a great deal of the wool sold in the UK is imported. Imports worth £5 million come from Australia where the barbaric mutilation known as mulesing is performed routinely: folds under the lamb's tail are sliced away, literally shearing the skin and flesh around the tail in order to discourage blow flies from depositing their eggs. The reason for this operation is that it is cheaper and requires less skill than the alternative of shearing carefully around the tail.[11]

ENTERTAINMENT

Although savage customs such as cock-fighting and bear-baiting have long been outlawed, animals are still used to provide us with entertainment. Some forms are more barbaric than others: for instance, it is hard to imagine any vegetarians who would condone the hunting of any animal for sport, but what about horse- or greyhound-racing? Then there are circuses which demand that wild creatures are kept incarcerated in a limited space, most of them subject to the continuous stress of transportation from one town to another. What makes both hunting and circuses with animals even more indefensible is that alternatives to both do exist. Drag-hunting can result in all the fun of the chase without the sordid barbarism of the kill; circuses without animals allow us to marvel at the skill of jugglers and acrobats without the degradation inflicted upon wild creatures.

The claims made by zoos that they have an educative value have surely long been undermined by the marvellous films of wild animals in their natural habitat which now exist. No person with a healthy respect for life would want to stare at a polar bear in a bare cage when film of these awesome creatures in their natural habitat is readily available. Nowadays, zoos are forced to defend themselves more on the grounds that they are valuable for conservation purposes, but this is also a dubious justification. Organizations like Zoo Check have shown a better way forward. Faced with the possible extinction of the black rhinoceros (only an estimated 300 remain), this organization has helped to create a rhino sanctuary in Kenya, enclosed by special solar-powered rhino fencing to provide a non-injurious barrier, closely guarded to protect the rhinos from poachers. Although there may be occasions when the only possibility of conserving a species is to keep it confined for a limited period until natural conditions more conducive to its survival are promoted, it is surely much more beneficial to preserve natural habitat than to keep animals alive in artificial conditions. After all, if no wild areas remain, then there will never be land available where we can return those species 'saved' by zoos. Simply to preserve species in prison-like confinement or in sperm banks, demonstrates more human conceit than any genuine interest in animal life.

PETS

There are no easy answers to the question of where the borders of living without cruelty to animals should be drawn. Nothing illustrates this statement more readily than the issue of pets. Sometimes a source of valuable companionship, consolation and affection to humans and often treated with love and respect, these same animals consume massive amounts of other slaughtered animals, ranging from meat from abattoirs and knackers' yards to wild creatures such as kangaroos. Furthermore, due to human negligence the problem of unwanted and neglected pets is an increasing burden. Does this mean that vegetarians should be against the keeping of pets? Even if we answer 'no', should we at least ensure that we choose stray and rejected animals rather than buy from the pet-breeding industry? In addition, should we place our pets on vegetarian diets? With dogs this need not create a problem for they can receive all the necessary nutrients but although there is now a vegetarian cat food available in the USA (Vegecat), there remains a considerable doubt whether our feline friends can be satisfied on a non-carnivorous diet.

A further problem created by the pet industry is that it offers another source of profits to the drug companies. Many of the firms involved in the production of drugs for the human market also produce goods for 'animal health', with all the innoculations, wormers, boosters, etc. themselves tested upon animals. There are those who believe that it is more advantageous to treat companion animals mainly through homoeopathic or herbal treatment, while it is widely recognized that a daily intake of garlic mixed in feed is an extremely effective cruelty-free preventative measure. For those who want to pursue the subject of herbal treatments for animals further the *Complete Herbal Handbook for Dogs and Cats* by Juliette de Bairacli Levy[13] is recommended.

FISH

Consumption of fish is usually justified on two grounds: first, it is presented as a healthy food; and second, it is argued that fish are unable to feel pain. On health grounds, there may have been little evidence in the past to guard against the consumption of seafood. Nowadays, however, the pollution of our waters with nuclear, industrial and agricultural waste and sewage has greatly undermined any such assertions.

The second of these defences has also been completely disproved recently. In 1980, an investigation by experts led to the publication of what is now known as *The Medway Report*. After three years spent examining all existing information, they found conclusive evidence that fish feel pain like other vertebrates. Consequently, the production of food by methods which include sticking baited hooks into the mouths of living creatures is unlikely to meet with approval from anyone concerned with a humane diet. *The Medway Report* shows that 'any hook causes tissue damage when it catches and thus, in medical terms inflicts an injury'.[14] The *Report* also stated that 'the tissues of a fish, when it is removed from water, are subject in air to pressure greatly reduced and differing in nature from those they are subject to in water. . . . Bleeding tends to occur from the gills'. It should also be remembered that if it was not for human greed in the fishing industry, there would be no lame excuses for the mass slaughter of dolphins or seals—creatures whose main 'crime' is to compete with humans for seafood.

CONCLUSION

The type of summary I have attempted in this chapter, while having its use in demonstrating the maxim that behind almost every product lies animal suffering, also possesses one great danger: namely, that by suggesting how the 'living without cruelty' message may enforce endless reappraisal of our ideas, it may also leave the individual feeling helpless. 'I cannot possibly avoid all animal cruelty, so what is the point in avoiding anything', it may be argued. Such an attitude should be resisted. Everybody has to draw their own line in the fight against exploitation and to be congratulated on doing *something*. The important thing is to do whatever you can do and most importantly, continue to question whether it is possible to do more. Nobody can ever afford to become self-righteous, because in the modern world it is more or less impossible to avoid utilizing all products associated with animal suffering. Hidden by-products from the slaughter-house are everywhere. While it may be possible to avoid products such as lard, suet, dripping, tallow, stearates, glycerine, glycerol, keratin, pepsin, lactates, caseinates, animal albumin and lanolin, the animal ingredients in photographic film, gramophone records, rubber, ceramics, plastics, glue, motor-car fan belts, gaskets and tyres, anti-freeze and even roads themselves are rather more difficult to avoid contact with! 'Living without cruelty' to animals (or for that matter, humans) can have no absolute definition: there can be no absolute dogma representing *the* approved life-style. At present, it is probably not even a totally obtainable goal without becoming a hermit! Yet this in no way undermines its importance as an ideal which the world must work towards.

CHAPTER TEN

Parents and Children

As we saw early in Chapter 9, everywhere in modern life there are commercial interests waiting to feed upon our insecurities in order to create profits. Perhaps the most pertinent example of all is in the 'baby market': pertinent, partly because no market appeals more to human vulnerability than the one aimed at mothers looking after newborn children, and partly because it is yet another example of the way that animal suffering contributes to an area of life with which one is unlikely to associate it.

During their spell in hospital many mothers will be presented with 'Bounty bags', paid for by commercial companies and combining a minimum of useful information with a mass of advertising and free samples for a multitude of goods. Pages abound with creams, fabric softeners, washing powders, milk-formula foods, wet wipes and so on. Indeed, babies' bottoms alone seem to have become a phenomenal commercial growth market! First, wet wipes replaced water for cleaning and now wet wipes have progressed to become antiseptic wet wipes! 'Special' is the key word. We have special baby soaps, special baby creams with antiseptic, special washing powders, special fabric softeners and even scent products to make baby's nappies smell like 'spring flowers'. Nowadays, at each changing time, the average baby's bottom gets smeared with antiseptic wet wipes, greasy creams and then talcum powder. All of them contain chemicals of one sort or another and, rather than protecting the poor child from rashes, many mothers believe that the combination of these substances is more likely to promote them. Parents who have resisted the baby market have insisted that none of these products are really necessary. Water (and adequate drying) will do the job perfectly, for it is cleanliness, not chemicals, that prevent rashes. If protection of sore skin is necessary, vaseline can be used.

The waste and deception involved in these products is, in itself, reason for objection. More importantly, however, the animal suffering during their development is inexcusable. Almost all of them will have been subjected to the normal range of animal tests—skin tests, carcinogenicity and, where applicable, Draize eye-irritancy tests.

CHILDREN AND VEGETARIAN DIETS

Turning to the question of food for the vegetarian baby, there are no medical reasons whatsoever why either babies or growing children should not be fed exclusively on either a lacto-vegetarian or vegan diet. Lacto-vegetarianism seems to be almost completely accepted by the medical profession, although as yet there remains a certain amount of hostility from some of the more conservative members of the medical, health-care and midwifery professions to a vegan diet for children. Fortunately, there are now third-generation vegan children and fifth generation lacto-vegetarians alive and well and offering proof to the feasibility of these dietary regimes. In addition, although medical research on vegan diets for children is still limited, there have been several studies published. In 1979, Dr T. A. B. Sanders of the Department of Nutrition at Queen Elizabeth Hospital concluded that vegan diets were suitable provided that the mother eats a balanced diet during pregnancy, taking particular care to ensure adequate sources of vitamin D and B12 and also calcium. He found that most vegan mothers breast-feed their children well into the second year and that 'breast milk can meet all nutritional requirements of the infant for the first four to six months of life, provided that there is enough milk'. He added that 'breast milk is still an adequate food after that age provided that it is supplemented with a suitable weaning food such as a mixture of cereals and (cooked) soya flour'. The third stage was to introduce the child to a completely balanced diet of cereals, pulses, nuts, fruits and vegetables.[1]

In 1981, the same researcher, together with Rebecca Purves, conducted a survey on 23 vegan children aged between one and five. Yet again his conclusion was that 'provided sufficient care is taken, a vegan diet can meet all the nutritional requirements of the pre-school child'. The only sources of concern were over levels of vitamin B12 and calcium. The researchers pointed out that unless levels in breast milk are adequate it is necessary to ensure a supplement. Worries over calcium deficiency were due to the fact that cow's milk is the most normal source of this mineral among children. Nevertheless, even apart from Plamil soya milk there are numerous non-animal sources of calcium such as sesame seeds or tahini, soya flour, soya beans, dried figs, raw cabbage, cooked broccoli, sunflower seeds, almonds and raw cabbage. Although this does seem to be an area where vegan mothers must take care during pregnancy to ensure an adequate supply this does not invalidate the diet. Moreover, adaption to low calcium intakes is known to occur and children receiving low intakes have been shown to remain in positive balance.[2] Summarizing their investigations, the researchers were prepared to accept that a vegan diet was suitable provided that vegan parents have 'a good knowledge and understanding of the principles of nutrition and food preparation'.[2] The only notable differences found between vegan and other children was that the former tended to be slightly shorter and leaner, neither of which is a cause for concern.

In a more recent study in the USA at the Department of Nutrition and Food Sciences in Florida State University, much the same conclusions were reached, together with a further question mark over the zinc intake of vegetarians and vegans. In this study, researchers also constructed their own diet plan to ensure adequate nutrients for vegan children. Remembering that no diet is likely to be perfect, this plan proves that recommended daily allowances of all nutrients are possible from a non-meat diet (see Tables 10·1 and 10·2). The best general advice to be given to all mothers is to educate yourself as thoroughly as is possible during pregnancy. Several books are available. In particular, Rose Elliot's *Vegetarian Mother and Baby Book*[3] is recommended as a proven source of support, comfort and cookery inspiration for many vegetarian and vegan mothers. Advice is also available from both The Vegan Society and The Vegetarian Society (UK).

Given then that a vegetarian diet can provide all the essentials for a healthy child, what should babies be fed on? Obviously, for the first few weeks 'breast is best', mother's milk being the food intended by nature for infant humans. Although there are many infant milk formulas available based on cow's milk for those unable to feed their young, at the time of writing there is something of a problem for vegan mothers with the same difficulty. In the UK, the only fully vegetarian soya infant formula available is named Prosobee, produced by Mead Johnson, and available only on prescription. Medically speaking, the scarcity of soya-based infant formulas is unfortunate, because a comparative study into the effects of cow's milk and soya-based formula on the recovery rate of infants with acute diarrhoea has shown significant advantages in the soya.[4] Solid foods are not normally introduced into babies' diets for at least three months, usually longer. Unfortunately, the majority of baby foods on the market tend to include animal produce, though many of the major manufacturers do now include a vegetarian range. Indeed, vegetarian cheese- and egg-based products are common enough now to make any product list unnecessary. Neither does Table 10·3 catalogue all the vegan baby foods available, omitting those fruit deserts that add sugar to the

Table 10·1 Diet plans for the vegan child

Food group	Approximate serving size	Daily servings per age group		
		6 months–1 year	1–4 years	4–6 years
Bread	1 slice	1	3	4
Cereals (enriched)[1]	1–5 tbsp	½ (finely ground)	1	2
Fats	1 tsp	0	3	4
Fruits:				
Citrus	¼–½ cup	0	2 (juiced or chopped)	2
Other[2]	2–6 tbsp	3 (puréed)	2 (chopped)	3
Protein foods[3]	1–6 tbsp	2 (cooked and sieved)	3 (chopped)	3
Vegetables[4]:	¼–⅓ cup			
dark green/deep yellow leafy		¼ (cooked and puréed)	½ (chopped)	1
Other		½ (cooked and puréed)	1 chopped	1
Soy milk (fortified)	1 cup	3	3	3
Miscellaneous:				
Brewer's yeast[5]	1 tbsp	0	1	1
Molasses	1 tbsp	0	1	1
Wheatgerm	1 tbsp	0	Optional	Optional

1 Cereals include dry bulgur, corn flakes, wheat flakes, shredded wheat, enriched rice, millet, macaroni, brown rice, wheat berries.

2 Other fruits include avocado, apple, peach, banana, pear, berries, apricots and grapes. Dried fruit spreads include those made with dried peaches, apricots, raisins and figs.

3 Protein foods include nuts, nut butters, peanut butter, legumes, miso, seeds, seed butters and tofu. Legumes include soybeans, peanuts, black beans, black-eyed peas, pintos and split peas. Nuts include almonds, cashews, pignolia, walnuts, pecans and pistachios. Seeds include pumpkin sesame and sunflower. Nuts and seeds should be ground for the toddler. Nut milks may be made for older children but should not replace soya milk.

4 Deep yellow and dark green leafy vegetables include carrots, green peppers, broccoli, spinach and kale. Other vegetables include bean sprouts, potatoes, tomatoes, lettuce, cabbage, sweet corn, celery, snap beans, onions, cucumbers, beets and cauliflower. Bean sprouts include mung, soy and alfalfa. Potatoes include white potato and sweet potato, baked and boiled.

5 Nutritional yeast is not an appropriate food for the infant. The purine content may be greater than 150 mg/100 gm. Yeast does not naturally contain vitamin B12. Fortified products are available; the amounts of vitamin B12 vary.

Source: Department of Nutrition and Food Sciences, Florida State University.

Table 10-2 Proximate nutritive value of basic diet plans for vegan children (% RAD = percentage of recommended daily intake)

Age (year)	Energy		Protein		Riboflavin		Vitamin B12[2]		Vitamin D[3]		Calcium		Iron		Zinc	
	kcal	% RDA	gm	% RDA	mg	% RDA	µg	% RDA	µg	% RDA	mg	% RDA	mg	% RDA	mg	% RDA
0.5–1	891	94	28	155	0·75	125	1·8	120	7·4	74	579	107	14·1	94	5·9	118
1–4	1330	102	44	160	1·32	165	1·8	90	7·4	74	905	113	19·3	129	8·9	86
4–6	1592	94	48	160	1·46	146	1·8	72	7·4	74	960	120	21·4	214	9·6	96

1 The energy content of the diet could be substantially increased with more liberal use of dried fruits, cereals and nut butters.
2 The B12 content of the diet could be increeased with B12 supplements, fortified brewer's yeast or fortified cereal. Many packeted foods also include vitamin B12.
3 Vitamin D status is improved by exposure to sunlight and by the use of fortified margarines.
4 The zinc content of the diet could be increased by including wheatgerm, fortified cereals and brewer's yeast.

Source: Department of Nutrition and Food Sciences, Florida State University.

finished product. It is best to guard against the development of a sweet tooth right from the beginning!

Table 10·3 Baby foods suitable for vegan children

Company	Type of food	Vegan varieties
Boots	Instant baby food (Stage 1)	Savoury mixed vegetables
	Baby food in jars (Stage 1)	Mixed vegetable savoury variety
	Granulated infant food	Garden vegetable casserole Golden vegetable hotpot
	Instant baby food (stage 2)	Country vegetable bake
	Baby food in jars (Stage 2)	Savoury vegetable casserole
Cow & Gate	Trial-size ready-to-eat meals	Vegetable and rice casserole
	Ready-to-eat meals (Stage 1)	Apple dessert Apple and Banana Dessert Apple and Orange Dessert Fruit Delight Dessert
	Ready-to-eat meals (Stage 2)	Vegetable casserole with pasta Pineapple dessert plus those listed under Stage 1.
Heinz	Dessert jars	Apple Apple and banana

Table 10·3 (*Continued*)

Company	Type of food	Vegan varieties
		Apple and blackcurrant
		Apple and orange
		Fruit salad
		Pear and cherry
		Apple and apricot
		Apple and banana
		Apple and orange
		Apple and pear
		Just apple
		Mixed fruit
	Vegetable meal cans	Carrot and tomato
		Golden vegetable
		Mixed vegetable
		Spring vegetables
		Winter vegetable
Robinson	Infant meals	Mixed vegetable dinner
Beech-nut (Available only in selected health-food shops and chemists imported by Eliko Food Distributors from the USA)	Stage 1	Golden delicious applesauce
		Chiquita Bananas
		Sweet potatoes
		Bartlett pears
		Yellow cling peaches
		Squash
		Royal imperial carrots
		Green beans
		Peas
	Stage 2	Oatmeal with applesauce
		Applesauce and cherries
		Bartlett pears and pineapple

Table 10·3 (*Continued*)

Company	Type of food	Vegan varieties
		Garden Vegetables
		Fruit Dessert
		Mixed vegetable
		Apricots with pears and applesauce
		Applesauce and banana
		Mixed cereal with applesauce and banana
		Peas and carrots
		Prunes with pears
		Pears and applesauce
		Bananas with pears and applesauce
	Stage 3	Sweet potato
		Banana with pears and applesauce
		Apricot with pears and applesauce
Familia	Swiss baby food range	Dates and bananas
		No added sugar
		Original
Granose	Baby food organic	Bean and mushroom stew
		Vegetable with wholewheat noodles
		Spring vegetables with brown rice
		Spring vegetables with 7 cereals
		Carrots with

Table 10·3 (*Continued*)

Company	Type of food	Vegan varieties
		apples*
		Mixed vegetables
		Carrots and
		almond cream
		Apple with pear
		and natural
		vitamin C*
		7 cereals with
		fruit*

* Contains honey. Some vegans do not eat honey, which is, of course, an animal product.

SCHOOLCHILDREN

Later in life the pressure felt by mothers to conform to a society that consumes animal products is often transferred to the child. At school all vegetarian children may be made to feel uncomfortable both by reactionary teachers and contemporaries who jeer at their unusual diet. There is no easy answer to this problem. Much depends upon the strength of the child and the sympathy or lack of it from those in authority. Sometimes, of course, it can be the parents themselves who become the reactionaries. Many children in non-vegetarian families instinctively wish to abstain from meat products as soon as they realize that the skipping lambs and grazing cattle they see in the fields are the same creatures which end up as dead flesh on their dinner plates. There can be little doubt that the number of vegetarian children would rise substantially if the instinct to boycott meat was not suppressed by some parents who insist upon feeding animal produce, partly for selfish, convenience reasons and partly because of the misguided idea that only meat will allow proper health and development.

Rather than being discouraged in schools, greater

dependence upon well-balanced vegetarian meals should be promoted. At present the diet fed to our children is disastrous, as revealed by the 1986 *Report to Government on the Food Consumed by Children at Schools*. Sugar and saturated fat intake are far too high and deficiencies in several essential vitamins and minerals are common.[5] The consequences of a bad diet at school age are impossible to establish because they do not show themselves until later in life. Dr R. W. D. Turner, an authority on the dangers of fats, has written that 'the present excessive use of whole milk and other animal fats is laying the foundations for future arteriosclerosis. Post-mortems on children killed accidentally show that most already have signs of arterial damage caused by over consumption of saturated fat'.[6] The main problem is that the meals eaten by children are almost entirely lacking in the B group of vitamins, vitamin C and fibre. Chips, burgers and sweets are a lethal combination and it is ludicrous that children are provided even with the choice of eating such products at school. Low-cost, easy-to-cook, good-quality, nutritional food could be provided at schools, with a greater emphasis laid on vegetarian food so that children are educated from an early age to discover the value of discriminatory eating, e.g. thick lentil and vegetable soup (213 millilitre), wholemeal bread (50 grams) with low-fat margarine, peanut butter (25 grams) and pickle, mixed peanuts and raisins (25 grams) and a glass of orange juice (150 millilitres) would provide more than adequate levels of protein and energy, minimal amounts of saturated fats and sugar, one-third of the daily requirements of vitamins A, B, C and D and also calcium and iron. As Hannah Wright puts it in her book, *Swallowing it Whole*, 'children quite like this kind of food and would like it even more if they were involved at an early age in discussion and choice concerning school lunch'.[7]

There are hopeful signs. Several local education authorities, such as Nottingham, Sheffield and Avon, have introduced wholefood school-lunches, inevitably involving more vegetarian food. In Avon, an estimated 20% of meals sold to children are vegetarian.[8] The Gallup Poll commissioned by The Realeat Company (VegeBurgers) shows that the single highest category of vegetarians is students aged 16 and over, 11% of whom are non-meat eaters. Furthermore, a smaller survey commissioned in secondary schools in Oxfordshire, undertaken on behalf of Realeat by Oxford Polytechnic, suggests that figures are likely to rise even more.[8] If local education authorities can provide a healthy eating programme, the spread of vegetarianism will, undoubtedly, be rapid.

From both an economic and health point of view, nutrition education is vital. A reduction in the burden on our NHS is one key reason why the diet provided for our children must improve. Who can deny that vegetarian food will play an essential part in the fight against debilitating disease?

GROWN-UPS!

Much has already been written about how adult vegetarians and vegans balance their diet to ensure sufficient intake of protein, carbohydrates, vitamins, minerals and fats. Any detailed guide here is unnecessary, particularly as there is no actual reason for any special advice. The old myth about vegetarians not getting enough protein has long been dispelled, and as one expert puts it, 'protein complementarity, endlessly discussed by many vegetarians, is an unnecessary practice for ordinary human nutrition'.[9] Similarly, Dr Jill Davis of South London Polytechnic nutrition department (not herself a vegetarian) has stated that 'people often speak defensively about vegetarianism and a lot of nonsense is talked about vitamin deficiency.'[10]

There has been a good deal of worry about the lack of B12 in the vegan diet, much of which seems to be unjustified. Although lack of B12 can lead to the extremely serious condition of pernicious anaemia, it must be recognized that stores in the body are considered sufficient for at least four years. In addition, test studies indicate that some vegans live between 14 and 17 years without a recognized source of B12, yet maintain normal serum levels. This indicates that the major problem may be caused by absorption rather than levels of intake. In this case, meat-eaters may be just as much at risk.

If you are concerned about sources of B12, it is fortunate that commercial foods for the vegan market now do include B12 in varying quantities. As well as yeast extract, some soya milks (notably Plamil), grape nuts, several varieties of textured soya protein and vegetarian sausage mix and some margarines all include quantities. Check contents before purchasing if you wish to ensure a B12 supplement.

Other excellent sources of B12 include tempeh (a traditional Japanese, fermented soya product) and, in particular, spirulina, a blue-green algae which grows on the surface of alkaline lakes. This remarkable food source contains twice the quantity of B12 as liver, from which most meat eaters obtain their supplies. It is also rich in several other vital nutrients. Finally, B12 tablets are available, though provided that care is taken with the diet they should not be necessary.

CHAPTER ELEVEN

Shopping Guide

As numbers have increased, shopping has become progressively easier for vegetarians. Nowadays, even some chain stores cater for the growing minority, providing a small range of products exclusively for lacto-vegetarians and sometimes one or two for vegans. Nevertheless, although there is no doubt that this trend will develop further in the next few years, at the moment the selection is still limited and vegetarians have to depend largely upon their local wholefood or health-food shop.

In this chapter, in which I will discuss some of the foods available, emphasis will be put upon those products which might be considered unusual or unconventional, since it would seem pointless to discuss cheese- and egg-based cookery or the more obvious convenience foods, such as vegetable soups or pizzas, at great length. All of the items mentioned can be obtained at most good wholefood shops. As stated previously, for many people vegetarianism means more than simply refusing to consume meat or rejecting all animal produce. Rather, it means living as self-sufficiently as possible and consuming a minimum of the world's resources. Some of those who adhere to this philosophy create as much of their own food as they can from raw ingredients: preparing their own meals, baking their own bread, cakes and biscuits and growing their own vegetables wherever possible. Others reduce or eliminate all dependence upon the food industry, which they view largely as a source of corruption and ill-health. Admirable though these sorts of life-style may be, it has also to be recognized that many others lack either the inclination or sufficient time to spend long periods in the kitchen or on the allotment and wish to conform to the modern trend for fast food. For this reason, the growing number of vegetarian convenience products will also be discussed.

IS VEGETARIANISM CHEAPER?

Vegetarians are often asked if their diet is cheaper than that of meat-eaters. Vegetarians eat crops that are grown directly for human consumption; meat-eaters eat what is basically vegetable protein passed inefficiently through animals in order to obtain a more 'luxurious' and expensive finished product. If you compare the low price of, for example, a pound of soya beans or lentils to the cost of a pound of minced beef or lamb, you will see the obvious truth of this statement. On the other hand, if you rely mainly upon vegetarian convenience foods, many items may prove to be a little more expensive than their meat equivalents. There are several reasons for this. Most importantly, the nutritional quality of vegetarian 'fast food' tends to be superior, utilizing good-quality fats, raw ingredients and natural flavourings.

The other reasons why vegetarian 'fast food' may be a little more expensive, though related to the above, have little to do with nutrition. Instead, they are the result of commercial considerations. As vegetarian food is not consumed on the same massive scale as meat products, both producers and retailers are usually relatively small companies, unable to indulge in either the chief mass-production methods or the cut-throat selling techniques of big suppliers or supermarket chain stores. In a free-market economy, minorities will almost inevitably have to pay a wider profit margin to producers.

In conclusion then, the more you depend upon convenience products, the more you will erode what is essentially a considerable margin in price between vegetarian food and animal produce. Yet this is only half the story, because it must be remembered that even if you do decide to buy fast vegetarian food you will most likely be purchasing a healthier, better-quality product than the meat equivalent.

PULSES AND NUTS

I will deal first with the vegetarian staples: pulses and nuts. Any combination of hazel-nuts, walnuts, cashews, Brazils, almonds and peanuts (the latter two to a lesser extent) are rich sources of protein and can be eaten raw in salads, as snacks or ground in any combination to form the basis of nut roast or rissoles. The most popular pulses are red kidney beans (these must be boiled for 15 minutes during cooking to destroy toxins), aduki beans, black-eyed beans, haricot beans, chick peas, butter beans, split peas and green, brown and red lentils.

The main problem that some people encounter with pulses is that they do require planning. Many of them need to be soaked overnight before cooking and may then take between one and two hours extra before they soften. If you are not very organized or simply do not have time, there are ways around the difficulties. First, you can obtain a pressure cooker. Second, when in a desperate hurry, some pulses can be purchased in tins (although this is expensive, they often contain added sugar and salt and they cannot be recommended on ecological grounds). Third, not all pulses require prolonged cooking. For instance, red lentils do not have to be soaked and will soften within 15 minutes. These make a delicious and nutritious addition to soups and stews. Black-eyed beans take only a little longer, particularly if they can be soaked for half an hour or so beforehand. Green and brown lentils will also cook within half an hour if soaked for a couple of hours beforehand. For many vegetarians beans provide the alternative to meat in a series of 'traditional' meat dishes. A combination of green and brown lentils can form the basis of a delicious shepherd's pie, black-eyed beans can be used in lasagne and aduki beans and wheat combined in a vegetarian hot-pot.

WHOLEMEAL GRAINS

These are an important part of most vegetarian diets. Used in association with the amino acids found in pulses, they form an ideal combination of protein, e.g. aduki beans and wheat; rice and black-eyed beans. Apart from the obvious grains such as brown rice, wholemeal macaroni, spaghetti and other pasta, you could try barley, oats, bulgar wheat, millet, buckwheat or rye.

MEAT SUBSTITUTES

Soya beans were not mentioned amongst the list of popular pulses, partly because they require such a long cooking period and also because of their tendency to cause flatulence. Nevertheless, soya is an important food, especially as the basic ingredient of textured vegetable protein (TVP), a component of so many vegetarian convenience foods. Soya is heated to a very high temperature and then produced either as mince or chunks. This is a process no more unnatural (though less traditional) than that by which we obtain flour from wheat, in that unlike much of the processing carried out by the modern-day food industry, it does not destroy the nutritional qualities of the original crop, it merely makes it more palatable.

Some vegetarians disapprove of these products, maintaining that it is wrong even to attempt to imitate meat and also objecting to the presence of chemicals in some flavoured TVP, although many of the products utilize only natural flavourings. Other vegetarians, particularly amongst the newly converted, base much of their cooking around it. Where TVP does seem particularly useful is in providing vegetarian meals for meat-eaters with a particularly conservative taste in food, many of whom have consumed a soya-bean pie under the impression that they were eating beef!

CONVENIENCE MAIN MEALS

Yet again, the purist will no doubt disapprove, but the desperately busy (or lazy) will be pleased to find an increasing range of convenience foods available in tins, packets and ready-to-eat for the freezer.

Granose Ltd is the company producing the largest range of tinned vegetarian foods. Reaction to these depends much upon individual taste. Responses differ greatly, so if you make a 'bad' choice at first, do not automatically condemn the whole range! Among the most popular items are meatballs, Mexican chilli beans, savoury bake (vegetarian meat pie) and nuttolene, which could best be described as a superior variation on luncheon meat made solely from peanuts and ready to serve cold from the tin, normally with salad. The latter two are suitable for vegans. Whole Earth Foods, best known for their peanut butters, delicious sugar-free jams and salad dressings, also market appetizing chilli, stir-fry brown rice and vegetables and sugar-free baked beans, all in tins.

Several firms produce meals in packet form, the ingredients of which are dehydrated. Water is added and the contents cooked through before serving. Choices include; goulash, chilli and bolognese from Hera; various soya-based recipes from Direct Foods Ltd; and falaffels by Fantastic Foods. Granose Ltd also make a number of dry-mix 'roasts' to which water is added before baking in the oven. These tasty meals include nut roast, sunflower and sesame, lentil and Mexican grain.

As with any shopping, the golden rule when trying any vegetarian convenience food is always to check the ingredients to ensure that: (a) they do not include any dubious additives or oils; and (b) that they are 100% vegetarian or, if preferred, vegan.

BURGERS AND BANGERS

Vegetarians are now spoilt for choice in this area. Several alternatives exist, all with one feature in common: namely, that they are lower in saturated fats than their meat equivalent. By far the biggest-selling products are VegeBurgers and VegeBangers, marketed by The Realeat Company. Like most other vegetarian sausages and burgers, they are sold packeted as a dried mix, to which water (and/or an egg or a few oats) are added before frying. Made from a combination of sesame seeds, grains, vegetables and herbs, VegeBurgers contain more protein, half the fat and fewer calories than an equivalent-sized meat burger. The Vege-Burger utilizes soya rather than sesame seeds and contains 30% more protein than it does vegetable fat. By contrast, the average pork sausage contains 75% more animal fats (saturated) than it does protein.

Many other vegetarian burgers and bangers available are also based upon soya. Although it is always advisable to check labels before purchasing, it is almost exclusively true that the ingredients are natural (where colouring is used in vegetarian sausages it is usually only beetroot powder) and the fat content is comparatively low. Among convenience dry-mix burgers and bangers are Sosfry, Sosmix, Hera Burgers, Burgamix and Savormix. Also available direct from the freezer are tofu burgers, nut burgers and sausage rolls ready prepared.

IN THE FREEZER

Apart from the above, the freezer department is likely to be of greater interest to the lacto-vegetarian than the vegan. Cheese made from animal-free rennet, goat's milk, margarine, yoghurt and additive-free ice cream made from milk taken from the Loseley Jersey-cow herd are among the most obvious examples. Incidentally, commercial cheeses not using animal rennet include Philadelphia (Kraft Ltd), Rowntree's Cheddar Spread and Safeway's cottage cheese, plain, with pineapple or with cheddar and onion.

Vegans may well find tofu the most valuable freezer food. Tofu is a curd made from soya beans and is part of the traditional Far Eastern cuisine. Although full of protein, it is also very bland and can absorb the flavour of almost any other ingredient. The curd can be sliced, mashed, deep fried or puréed and is used in both sweet and savoury dishes. There are numerous margarines suitable for lacto-vegetarians on the market, but at the time of writing only Granose, Vitaquell, Suma, Pure, Meridian and Vitasieg contain no animal products. A recent luxury addition to the vegan food market is ice cream containing soya rather than dairy produce. The Tofu Company, Vive, Dayville, Sunrise and Hera now market various flavours, although some do include honey. They are expensive but very tasty!

SAVOURY SPREADS AND FLAVOURINGS

Yeast extract is a particularly valuable food. It adds flavour to stews, soups and casseroles or can be eaten as a spread. Some brands are also a source of vitamin B12. Vecon, Barmene, Tastex, Community Foods' yeast extract, Natex, Meridian and Marmite all include the vitamin. All differ slightly in taste. Vegetarian pâtés are also popular for sandwiches and come in various flavours. Granose Ltd, the Tofu Company and Vessen all market pâtés. Perhaps the most well-known, however, is Tartex.

Tahini is a paste made from sesame seeds. It can be used either as a spread or in traditional Near Eastern dishes such as houmous. Peanut butter is the best known of the nut spreads. The brands available in wholefood shops are normally more expensive than those in supermarkets, mainly because they contain more peanuts and, unlike many of the latter, no added sugar. Some contain salt. There are also now spreads available made from sunflower seeds, cashews, almonds, hazel-nuts and tofu. All of these make an interesting change in sandwiches.

Other products based upon the soya bean may be unfamiliar to new vegetarians. Soya sauce or shoyu (fermented soya beans), miso (a paste made from fermented soya beans), tempeh, tabasco sauce and tamari (fermented soya bean with wheat) are wonderful sources of flavour for soups, stews or vegetables, although they should be added sparingly. Some of the cheaper varieties include monosodium glutamate, so it is best to choose a more expensive brand.

FLOUR

Most vegetarians will prefer to purchase wholewheat flour, both for the high fibre content and for the greater quantities of protein. Many brands are available, though Doves' Organic Flour is recommended as the most readily available brand produced without the use of artificial fertilisers.

Wholefood shops also sell flour obtained from chick peas (gram flour), soya, rice, potatoes and other grains. Apart from being highly nutritious, these all offer different flavours to sauces, biscuits, etc.

BEAN SPROUTS

Sprouted beans or seeds are a rich source of vitamin C and give flavour and a crispy texture to salads or stir-fry vegetables. They can also be boiled. Mung beans, alfalfa seeds and sprouted lentils are among the most popular. Special sprouting equipment can be purchased from some health-food shops but is not strictly necessary. A small pot (not glass) covered with a piece of muslin and stored in a warm place is sufficient. All you have to do is soak two tablespoonfuls of beans overnight in tepid water and cover them with muslin. The next morning, rinse them and strain off the water, leaving the beans damp but not lying in water. Repeat this exercise two or three times a day for the next two or three days, after which the beans will have sprouted and will be ready for eating.

BISCUITS

Many of the bigger commercial companies include animal fats in their products, mainly because they are cheaper. Luckily, the picture is now changing and there are now plenty of varieties suitable for lacto-vegetarians on the market. For vegans, the choice is not so good because the cheap price and wide availability of dairy by-products, such as whey and dried milk powder, from the EEC milk lakes encourages manufacturers to utilize them for flavouring. Health-food shops do now sell several brands of vegan biscuits including Allinsons (some varieties). Braycot, Mitcheldene, Doves (with honey) and Northumbria. Of the larger companies, McVities Natural Choice range and Fox's ginger biscuits are all suitable for vegans. Marks and Spencer and Sainsburys also sell a number of items free from animal fats. Keep checking the labels for new discoveries!

PUDDINGS AND CONFECTIONERY

Once again, lacto-vegetarians have a much wider choice than vegans. Therefore desserts totally free from animal produce deserve a special mention. Both Provamel and Granose market a vanilla-, carob- or strawberry-flavoured soya desert (a sort of vegan blancmange). Plamil Foods Ltd are responsible for a rice pudding with soya milk and sultanas: it is made from organic, unpolished rice and makes a delicious, creamy and filling pudding. All goods available from Plamil Foods Ltd are suitable for vegans. These include both a chocolate and a carob bar with soya milk.

Carob, made from the carob bean, is used as an alternative to chocolate and is also a source of iron and calcium.

As well as forming the basis of some vegetarian confectionery, it can be produced as flour and taken in drinks (hot carob, carob shakes) or used in cooking.

Every month the number of confectionery bars available at health-food shops increases, so the only real advice is to look closely at the labels and try them out.

SETTING AGENTS

Vegetarians are unable to eat the majority of commercial jellies or other products because they include gelatine as a setting agent, which is obtained from the feet and hooves of slaughtered animals. It is also used in the casing of many vitamin pills. The most common vegetarian alternative is agar agar and can normally be found in health-food stores. Other vegetable gums can also be bought, as can instant jelly mixes.

The above guide lists some of the most popular foods in the vegetarian kitchen, but it is by no means a comprehensive list. New products and companies are proliferating onto the market all the time with vegetarian alternatives. There are salad creams, sauces, soup, crisps, crispbreads, ketchups, gravies and cakes, as well as variations on the goods already described. We have also taken no heed of the many popular convenience foods which are vegan, such as Heinz' baked beans.

Eating out has also become much easier: almost every town has at least one restaurant catering for vegetarians. Even vegans are finding alternatives to beans, chips and peas at the local fish and chip shop. However, a visit to the local 'chippy' can be fraught with difficulty. Check that they cook in vegetable oils rather than animal fats.

All this represents a tremendous change in a short space of time. Only five years ago, shopping and eating out presented something of a problem. Within the next five years, it is unlikely that there will be any limitations at all, for there seems little doubt that almost every large chain store will be catering for the increasing vegetarian and vegan markets.

Part Two

Recipes for Change

Introduction

The fact that there are many serious and compelling reasons for human beings to adopt vegetarianism should not lead the reader to believe that adopting an animal-free diet is simply a question of self-sacrifice. On the contrary, one of the greatest benefits of vegetarian food is that it is significantly more tasty, varied and interesting than a meat-based diet. Indeed, T. A. B. Sanders, whose scientific studies I have referred to several times in the text, has written that 'although it is widely held that vegan and vegetarian diets are restricted, most British vegans and vegetarians consume a very wide variety of plant foods. Indeed their diets tend to contain more variety than that of the typical non-vegetarian. Consequently, the term omnivore (one who eats anything) to describe a non-vegetarian is a misnomer'[1].

The recipes prepared for this book by Sarah Brown have been chosen specifically to illustrate both the range and flexibility of vegetarian food. The majority of people would believe it impossible to create cakes, quiches, roasts, pasties, white sauces or what are thought to be traditional meat dishes, such as moussaka, without using any meat or dairy produce. Yet none of the dishes here contains animal produce. As an introduction, they prove that vegetarian cooking is far from restrictive, can be as elaborate or as simple and as quick as you wish it to be and can draw upon a wide range of traditions—from the British 'roast and two veg' idea to the many different cultures which now enrich our society.

All this, in addition to being both delicious and healthy!

141

Butter Bean Moussaka

2 onions, peeled and finely chopped
1 tbsp olive oil
1 clove garlic, crushed
1 bay leaf
1 tsp basil
1 tsp thyme
½ tsp nutmeg
8 oz (125 g) butter beans (cooked weight)
1 × 14 oz (400 g) tin tomatoes
2 tbsp tomato purée
1–2 tbsp shoyu
salt and pepper
2 large potatoes, boiled and sliced
1 large aubergine
¼ pint (150 ml) soya milk sauce (see recipe for *Creamy White Sauce* below).
1–2 tbsp sesame seeds

Gently fry the onions in the oil until soft. Add the garlic, herbs, spice and butter beans and cook gently for several minutes. Add the tomatoes and purée and then simmer for 30 minutes. Season with shoyu, salt and pepper.

Meanwhile prepare the potatoes. Slice the aubergine thickly and then fry two or three slices at a time for 3–5 minutes on either side. To finish the moussaka, put layers of the tomato sauce, aubergine and potato in a lightly greased, ovenproof dish. Finish with a layer of potato. Cover with the creamy soya milk sauce and sprinkle with sesame seeds. Bake at gas mark 5, 375°F (190°C) for 35–40 minutes.

Versatile Nut Roast

Although the butt of many vegetarian jokes, a nut roast is a quick and tasty dish to make. It can be adapted to suit many occasions, from a festive one to a family supper. Make plenty as it is delicious cold the next day in the best roast tradition! The main point with cooked nut mixtures is that they need to be moist and very well flavoured; otherwise the end result will be leaden and bland.

½ oz (10 g) sunflower margarine
1 small onion, peeled and finely chopped
4 oz (110 g) mushrooms, wiped and diced
1 tsp rosemary
1 tsp thyme
½ tsp nutmeg
2 tsp wholewheat flour
¼ pint (150 ml) red wine and ¼ pint (150 ml) dark
    vegetable or bean stock OR ½ pint (275 ml) stock
1 tsp yeast extract
1 tbsp tomato purée
4 oz (110 g) walnuts, ground or very finely chopped
2 oz (50 g) unsalted peanuts, ground
5 oz (150 g) breadcrumbs
1–2 tbsp tahini
1–2 tbsp shoyu
pepper

Melt the margarine and gently fry the onion until soft. Add the mushrooms, herbs and spice and cook for 5 minutes in a covered pan. Sprinkle over the flour and cook for 2 minutes. Add the wine, stock, yeast extract and tomato purée. Bring to the boil stirring constantly and cook for 5 minutes.

In a separate bowl, mix the nuts and breadcrumbs. Add the mushroom mixture, tahini and shoyu. Mix well and season to taste. Pack into a well-greased loaf tin and bake for 40–45 minutes at gas mark 5, 375°F (190°C). The loaf should be quite firm to the touch. Serve with a savoury or mushroom sauce, green vegetable and baked or roast potatoes.

Almond Crumble

Nut milks and creams are delicious when used as sauces for vegetable crumbles or casseroles. The flavour is rich and the texture very smooth.

For the topping:
    4 oz (110 g) oatflakes
    2 oz (50 g) ground almonds
    1 small onion, minced
    1 tsp sage
    1–2 tbsp sunflower oil
    salt and pepper

For the filling:
    1 onion, peeled and finely chopped
    1 tbsp sunflower oil
    8 oz (225 g) carrots, scrubbed and diced
    8 oz (225 g) green beans, washed and diced
    2 sticks celery, chopped
    8 oz (225 g) parsnips, scrubbed and diced
    2 oz (50 g) blanched almonds, chopped
    4 oz (110 g) ground almonds
    up to ¾ pint (400 ml) pale vegetable stock
    salt and pepper

For the crumble, mix together the oatflakes, almonds, onions, sage and seasoning. Rub in the oil to coat all the ingredients.

For the filling, gently fry the onion in the oil until soft, add the vegetables and chopped almonds and stir in well. Then cover the pan and sweat the vegetables for 10 minutes. Mix the ground almonds with the vegetable stock to make a creamy sauce. Pour this over the vegetables and stir well.

Spoon the vegetable sauce into a lightly oiled casserole dish. Sprinkle over the topping. Bake at gas mark 5, 375°F (190°C) for 25–30 minutes. Serve hot.

Coconut Rice with Beansprouts and Banana Curry

Velvet-textured rice and a golden banana curry make a delicious quick meal. Serve with Indian breads and some cooling cucumber for an exotic supper.

For the rice:
   2 oz (50 g) creamed coconut
   ¾ pint (400 ml) boiling water
   8 oz (225 g) long-grain brown rice
   6 peppercorns, finely crushed

For the curry:
   4 cloves garlic
   ½ tsp salt
   ¼–½ tsp chilli powder
   2 tsp coriander
   ½ tsp turmeric
   1 tsp garam masala
   3 tbsp sesame and sunflower oil mixed
   2 onions, peeled and finely chopped
   1 large cauliflower
   4 bananas
   2 oz (50 g) beansprouts
   2 oz (50 g) sultanas

For the rice, grate the coconut and dissolve it in the water and then soak the rice in it for 30 minutes with the peppercorns. Bring the rice to the boil in the soaking water and simmer for 30–40 minutes or until soft. Add a little extra boiling water if necessary.

For the curry, mix the garlic and all the spices and salt together with a little water to make a paste. Heat the oil and gently fry the onion until soft. Add the spice paste and cook for several minutes. Then add the cauliflower and bananas and cook for 10 minutes. Add the beansprouts and sultanas and cook for a further 5 minutes. Serve hot, accompanied by the rice.

Summer Vegetable Quiche

This easy quiche can be adapted for any season of the year but always make sure it is brimful of tasty vegetables. When making wholewheat pastry, be sure to make a soft dough, and do not overwork the fat into the flour or it will become very sticky, making it difficult to judge the amount of water necessary.

For the pastry:
   4 oz (110 g) wholewheat flour
   pinch salt
   ½ tsp baking powder
   2 oz (50 g) vegetable fat
   1 tbsp sunflower oil
   2–3 tbsp cold water

For the filling:
   1 tbsp sunflower oil
   1 onion, peeled and finely chopped
   4 oz (110 g) mushrooms, diced
   8 oz (225 g) courgettes, diced
   8 oz (225 g) broccoli, in small fleurettes
   1 tbsp wholewheat flour
   1 tsp oregano
   1 pkt silken tofu
   1 clove garlic
   juice of ½ lemon
   salt and pepper
   2 tbsp sesame seeds

Mix together the flour, salt and baking powder and lightly rub in the vegetable fat. Add the oil and water and mix quickly to a soft dough. Wrap in polythene and rest in a cool place for 30 minutes. To make the filling, heat the oil and gently fry the onion for 3 minutes. Add the vegetables and cook for a further 5 minutes. Then add the flour and oregano and cook for 1 minute. Remove from

146

the heat. Blend together the tofu, garlic and lemon juice until smooth and season to taste. Mix the tofu with the cooked vegetables.

Roll out the pastry to fill an 8 inch (20·5 cm) flan ring. Press in well and prick all over. Bake for 4 minutes at gas mark 6, 400°F (200°C). Spoon in the filling and sprinkle with sesame seeds. Bake for 30–35 minutes or until the tofu has set and the pastry is cooked.

Tofu Tostadas

This easy vegetable sauce is made into a delicious meal by adding the tasty cornmeal topping. Do make sure the oven is pre-heated, and once the topping is mixed, bake it straight away; otherwise the baking powder will not work as well.

For the sauce:
    1 onion, peeled and finely chopped
    1 tbsp sunflower oil
    2 cloves garlic
    2 sticks celery, diced
    1 large green pepper
    1 large red pepper
    8 oz (225 g) firm tofu, diced
    1 tsp cumin seed
    2 tsp marjoram
    2–3 drops tabasco sauce
    2–3 tbsp tomato purée
    1–2 tsp miso, dissolved in a little water
    salt and pepper

For the topping:
    3 oz (75 g) wholewheat flour
    3 oz (75 g) cornmeal
    1 oz (25 g) sunflower seeds
    1 tsp baking powder
    ½ tsp salt
    2 tbsp sunflower oil
    up to ¼ pint (150 ml) soya milk

For the sauce, gently fry the onion for several minutes in the oil and then add the garlic, celery, peppers, tofu, cumin and marjoram. Sweat the vegetables for 10 minutes. Add the tabasco sauce, tomato purée and miso and cook the sauce for a further 10 minutes. Season well and spoon into a lightly greased dish.

For the topping, mix together the flour, cornmeal, sunflower seeds, baking powder and salt. Mix in the oil and soya milk to make a soft, rough dough. Either cut into rounds and place on top of the vegetable sauce or spread over the top. Bake in a hot oven gas mark 6, 400°F (200°C) for 20–25 minutes.

Hazelnut and Spinach Pasties

A spinach purée makes an excellent filling for pasties, pies or pancakes. Here, it is mixed with hazel-nuts and flavoured with the aromatic spice cumin. The filling is quite crumbly; for a more solid mixture add 1–2 tbsp tahini.

Makes 10–12 pasties

For the flaky pastry:
    6 oz (175 g) solid vegetable fat
    8 oz (225 g) wholewheat flour
    pinch salt
    ¼ pint (150 ml) cold water
    squeeze lemon juice

For the filling:
    1 lb (450 g) spinach, thoroughly washed
    1 tbsp olive oil
    1 onion, peeled and finely chopped
    1 clove garlic, crushed
    1 tsp cumin seed
    6 oz (175 g) hazel-nuts, finely ground
    2 oz (50 g) breadcrumbs
    2 tbsp parsley
    1–2 tsp shoyu
    pepper

Chill the fat for at least 30 minutes before making the pastry. Mix the flour and salt in a large mixing bowl and quickly grate in the fat. Then add the water and lemon juice to make a rough dough. Cover with polythene and chill for 30 minutes. Roll into an oblong strip, fold in the top third, then the bottom third, seal the edges and give the pastry a quarter turn clockwise. Repeat twice and then chill again for 30 minutes.

To make the filling, chop the spinach finely and cook for 5–6 minutes without adding extra water. Cool and purée roughly. Heat the oil and gently fry the onion, garlic and cumin seed. Remove from the heat and add the cooked spinach, hazel-nuts, breadcrumbs, parsley and shoyu. Mix well and season to taste.

Roll out the flaky pastry and cut out 10–12 circles. Put a spoonful of filling on each circle, seal up with water, and prick a hole in each side. Bake the pasties at gas mark 7, 425°F (220°C) for 15–20 minutes. Eat hot.

Creamy White Sauce

When making a roux with an oil or soft margarine, it is very important not to heat the fat too fiercely or the flour will be scorched when added. Soya milk makes a delicious creamy sauce to which you can add various flavourings, such as onion, parsley or mushrooms.

2 tbsp sunflower oil OR 1 oz (25 g) sunflower margarine
1 oz (25 g) wholewheat flour
½ pint (275 ml) soya milk
pinch mustard powder
salt and pepper

Gently heat the oil or melt the margarine. Sprinkle over the flour and cook the roux for 1–2 minutes. Gradually add the milk, stirring constantly, and bring the sauce to boiling point. Simmer for 2–3 minutes. Add the mustard powder and season to taste.

Savoury Sauce

It is not difficult to make a good-flavoured sauce or gravy. The essential seasonings are miso and shoyu as they give a full-bodied taste but are also quite salty. A rich vegetable or bean stock will improve the sauce: use the water from cooking red kidney, black-eyed or aduki beans.

2 tbsp sunflower oil
1 onion, peeled and finely chopped
1 tsp celery seeds
1 carrot, peeled and finely diced
1 small white turnip, peeled and finely diced
4 oz (110 g) field mushrooms, diced
1 tbsp wholewheat flour
1 pint (570 ml) dark bean stock or vegetable stock
1 tbsp tomato purée
1 tbsp miso, dissolved in a little warm water
1–2 tsp shoyu
black pepper

Heat the oil and gently fry the onion and celery seed for 4 minutes. Add the vegetables, cover the pan and sweat them for 10 minutes. Add the flour and cook for 1 minute. Pour over the stock, add the tomato purée, and then, stirring constantly, bring the sauce to poiling point. Simmer for 5 minutes. Add the miso and shoyu and cook for a further 1 minute. Season to taste.

Tofu and Raisin Smoothie

Silken tofu is an ideal base for a 'smoothie', an American term for a creamy dessert. The combination of fruits, both fresh and dried, which you can use for flavouring are endless.

Serves 5

4 oz (110 g) seedless raisins
¼ pint (150 ml) apple juice
1 pkt silken tofu
1 banana (optional)
1 tsp carob powder
1 tbsp rum

For the garnish:
1 tbsp chopped nuts

Gently simmer the raisins in the apple juice for 30 minutes. Cool and drain. Blend all the ingredients until smooth. Serve chilled in tall glasses. Garnish with chopped nuts.

Orange Cake

Deceptively simple, these ingredients make a wonderful light cake. Do make the mixture wet for a good result. In order to ring the changes, use a lemon instead of the oranges.

10 oz (275 g) self-raising wholewheat flour
8 oz (225 g) brown sugar
2 oz (50 g) soya flour
1 tsp bicarbonate of soda
pinch salt
4 fl oz (110 ml) sunflower oil
juice of 2 oranges
1 tsp orange rind
1 tsp vanilla essence
extra orange juice or soya milk to mix

Mix the dry ingredients together. Mix the oil, orange juice, rind and vanilla essence together and then pour over the dry ingredients. Stir everything thoroughly and add extra orange juice or soya milk to make quite a wet mixture. Spoon into a well-greased 8 inch (20·5 cm) cake tin and bake at gas mark 4, 350°F (180°C) for 1–1¼ hours.

Part Three

Living Without Cruelty in Action

A Brief Summary

The problem with attempting any summary or guide to action for a book like this is that the scope is limitless. One of the chief objects has been to encourage people to make connections which they might otherwise not have made between animal, human and environmental abuse. Once the association is established, the ramifications are endless. The excuse, if one is needed, for not making the following summary as comprehensive as it might be is that while connections between vegetarianism and, for example, racism or feminism are there for the reader to develop, they are not crucial to the central thesis of this particular work. *Remember, it is only a guide and everybody must draw their own conclusions about which steps they feel able to take.*

FLESH FOODS

1 Eliminate completely.
2 If you really find this too difficult: (a) cut out all factory-farmed produce (chicken, pig meat and convenience meats in particular); and (b) reduce to a bare minimum and eliminate gradually.

EGGS

1 Eat only free-range eggs.
2 Reduce to a maximum of four per week.
3 Eliminate from the diet.

MILK

1 Try some of the various soya milks available.
2 Reduce levels as far as possible.
3 Eliminate.

CHEESE AND BUTTER

1 Buy vegetarian cheese only.
2 Reduce consumption.
3 Eliminate. For replacement foods see Chapter 4.
4 Replace butter with vegetable margarine, used sparingly (see Chapter 4).

Useful addresses

The Vegan Society, 33–5 George Street, Oxford, OX1 2AY

Animal Aid, 7 Castle Street, Tonbridge, Kent, TN9 1BH.

The Vegetarian Society, 53 Marloes Road, London W8 6LA.

Plamil Foods Ltd, Bowles Well Gardens, Folkestone, Kent, CT19 6PQ.

FRUIT AND VEGETABLES

1 Eat a wide variety.
2 Buy as much home-grown produce as you can: it is fresher and encourages self-sufficiency.
3 Boycott produce from nations whose political systems you oppose.
4 If possible support organic growers.
5 Write letters to supermarkets urging them to provide organic produce.
6 Consider taking an allotment or sharing one with friends.
7 If you do have an allotment, grow your food organically.
8 Try to buy organic seeds.

Useful addresses

Soil Association, 86 Colston Street, Bristol, BS1 5BB

The Organic Growers Association, Aeron Park, Llangeitho, Nr Tregaron, Dyfed, Wales.

Henry Doubleday Research Association, Ryton-on-Dunsmore, Coventry, Warwickshire.

Chase (UK), Organic Seeds, Coombelands House, Addlestone, Weybridge, Surrey KT15 1HY.

Veganic Garden Products, Gatehouse Cottage, Heath Farm Road, Worsted, Norfolk, NR28 9GH.

Useful books

A. Gear, *The New Organic Food Guide* (Dent, 1987).
K. D. O'Brien, *Veganic Gardening* (Thorsons, 1986).
L. Hills, *Organic Gardening* (Penguin, 1977).
G. Frack *Companion Planting* (Thomsons, 1983).

DRINKS

1 If you drink tea and coffee, purchase from organizations which guarantee a fair price plus decent working and living conditions for those who produce the crop.
2 When buying fruit juices, try to purchase those made with English or at least European produce. 'From more than one country' normally means from the Third World, grown as a cash crop.

Useful addresses

Traidcraft, Kingsway, Gateshead, South Shields, NE11 ONE.

World Development Movement, Bedford Chambers, Covent Garden, London, WC2E 3HA.

Oxfam, 274 Banbury Road, Oxford, OX2 7DZ. (Almost all Oxfam shops sell tea, instant and ground coffee).

GRAINS, PULSES, NUTS AND OTHER VEGETARIAN FOOD

1 Reduce dependence on vegetarian convenience foods.
2 Eat home-grown products as far as is possible (at present the range is limited).
3 Eat products that could at least be grown in this country.
4 Buy organic if it is at all possible.
5 Purchase only wholegrains.
6 Consider setting up a co-operative with friends and purchasing in bulk from wholesalers.
7 Buy from organizations guaranteeing a fair price and decent working conditions for the producers, e.g. Traidcraft.

Useful book
Health Food Buyers Guide Argos Publications [30 Street Approach, West Byfleet, Surrey], (1987/8) (Contains a full list of manufacturers.)

HOUSEHOLD WASTE

Whilst one half of the world starves, we squander resources.
1 Return all used and unwanted bottles and jars to your local bottle bank.
2 Urge your local council to also provide tin banks.
3 Try and find somewhere that recycles paper (sometimes local scout groups provide a service.) Purchase recycled paper when possible.
4 If you have a garden or allotment, save all waste matter for compost. (Oxfam estimate that 25% of food purchased by householders is thrown away.)
5 Separate your aluminium waste. Many Oxfam shops take it for recycling.

Useful address
Friends of the Earth, 377 City Road, London, EC1V 1NA.

Useful books
Friends of the Earth Handbook, (Optima Books, 1986).
J. Vogler *Recycling for Change* (Christian Aid).

HOUSEHOLD GOODS

1 Never buy anything labelled 'new', 'improved', 'advanced', etc. This is likely to mean newly tested on animals!
2 Rely upon traditional formulas (see Chapter 9).
3 Buy products known to be biodegradable and/or not tested on animals.
4 Learn which well-known commercial goods claim not to test their products on animals.
5 Use simple solutions, e.g. bleach and soda crystals, which will at the very least not have been tested on animals for many years.

Useful addresses
The Vegan Society, 33–5 George Street, Oxford, OX1 2AY. (The Society publishes *The Cruelty-Free Shopper* annually.)

Ecover Products, Full Moon, Charlton Court Farm, Steyning, Sussex, B94 3DF.

Caurnie Soap Company, Canal Street, Kirkintilloch, Glasgow, G66 1QZ. (The company markets disinfectant and washing-up liquid.)

Janco Sales, Dept. EV, 11 Seymour Road, Hampton Hill, Middlesex, TW12 1DD. (The company sells all-purpose washing liquid by mail order.)

Faith Products, 52–6 Albion Road, Edinburgh, EH7 5QZ. (The company produces Clear Spring liquid washing detergent and washing-up liquid.)

COSMETICS

1 Choose only cruelty-free products (i.e. those not tested on animals and not including animal derivatives).
2 If you cannot find a non-animal alternative do not use them.

Useful addresses
Pure Plant Producers, Grosvenor Road, Horlake, Wirral, Merseyside, L47 3BS.

Animal Aid Cruelty-free Cosmetics, 7 Castle Street, Tonbridge, Kent, TN9 1BH. (All profits go towards fighting animal abuse.)

Honesty Cosmetics, Bowling Green Craft Workshop, South Place, Chesterfield, Derbyshire, S40 1TA.

Faith Products, 52–6 Albion Road, Edinburgh, EH7 5QZ.

Tiki Cosmetics, Sisson Road, Gloucester, GL1 3QB.

The Body Shop (High Street shops all over the country.)

Weleda (UK) Ltd, Heanor Road, Ilkeston, Derbyshire, D67 8DR.

Camilla Hepper, Newton Road, Bovey Tracey, Devon, TQ13 9DX

Beauty without Cruelty, 37 Avebury Avenue, Tonbridge, Kent, TN9 1TL.

CLOTHING

1 Never wear fur.
2 Look for alternatives to leather and suede.
3 Try to replace wool.

Useful addresses
The Vegan Society, 33–5 George Street, Oxford, OX1 2AY (See *The Vegan Shopper's Guide.*)

LYNX, PO Box 509, Great Dunmow, Essex, CM6 1UH. (An anti-fur society.)

PETS

1 Determine whether you really need a pet. Consider helping friends look after theirs or taking joint responsibility if you are not sure. Alternatively, consider giving a home to an animal from a shelter or sanctuary.
2 Remember that small, imported animals in pet shops suffer dreadful transport conditions.
3 If you take a pet consider one that does not need to be caged.

4 Have your pet neutered. Do not breed unnecessarily as there are thousands of animals destroyed every year because they are unwanted.
5 Make sure you know how to care for your pet's needs: that it has adequate food, water and exercise and that it has proper medical attention when it requires it.
6 Do not give an animal as a present without discussing your intention with the prospective new owner.
7 If you have a dog, consider bringing it up on a vegetarian diet.*
8 Give your pet a daily dose of garlic and generally look into the feasibility of alternatives to drug therapies.

Useful addresses
The Royal Society for the Prevention of Cruelty to Animals, The Causeway, Horsham, West Sussex, RH12 1HG

Useful book
J. de Bairacli Levy *The Complete Herbal Handbook for Dogs and Cats* (Faber & Faber)

MEDICINES

1 For minor ailments either: (a) give your body rest and time to recover without medical intervention; or (b) buy homoeopathic, biochemic or other alternative remedies.
2 For more persistent symptoms consider alternative practices.
3 If you do decide to try alternatives try and find a doctor who prescribes homoeopathic cures on the NHS.
4 Even if you do decide to try orthodox medicine for a minor ailment do not take drugs unless you really need them: some doctors overprescribe.

* Happidog Pet Food, Bridgend, Longton, Preston, Lancs, PR4 4SJ. (Vegetarian dog food.)

Useful addresses

The Society of Homoeopaths, 2a Bedford Place, Southampton, SO1 2BY (These are registered practitioners and therefore not available on the NHS.)

The British Homoeopathic Association, (NHS doctors.) 27a Devonshire Street, London, W1N 1RJ.

The British Chiropractors Association, 5 First Avenue, Chelmsford, Essex, CM1 1RX.

British Naturopathic and Osteopathic Association, Frazer House, 6 Netherall Gardens, London, NW3.

The National Institute of Medical Herbalists, School of Herbal Medicine, 148 Forest Road, Tunbridge Wells, Kent, TN2 5EY.

The Nature Cure Clinic, 15 Oldbury Place, London, W1M 3AL.

Weleda (UK) Ltd, Heanor Road, Ilkeston, Derbyshire, D67 8DR (Homoeopathic medicines.)

Potters Herbal Supplies, Leyland Mill Lane, Wigan.

Useful book

A. Melville and C. Johnson *Alternatives to Drugs* (Fontana, 1987).

MEDICAL RESEARCH

While most medical charities do, alas, sponsor research involving animal use, the following organisations have stated that they do not (at the time of going to press). In addition, some specific projects for new machinery are 'safe' for anti-vivisectionists to support. Contact your area health authority for details.

Useful addresses

Quest for a Test for Cancer, Woodbury, Harlow Road, Roydon, Essex, CM19 5HF. (Searching for an early detection test for cancer, this organization is opposed to animal testing both on moral and scientific grounds.)

The British Cancer Control Society, 75 St Mary's Road, Market Harborough, Leicestershire, LE16 7DX.

Marie Curie Memorial Foundation, 28 Belgrave Square, London, SWX 82G. Although not opposed to animal work in principle, the Charity

166

closed down its animal experimentation laboratory in 1982 because of more exciting progress in non-animal techniques.)

Royal National Institute for the Deaf, 105 Gower Street, London, WC16 6AH.

Dr Hadwen Trust for Humane Research, 46 Kings Road, Hitchin, Herts, SG5 1RD (The Trust funds research which does not use animals.)

Humane Research Trust, 29 Bramhall Lane South, Bramhall, Cheshire, SK7 2DN.

Lord Dowding Fund, 51 Harley Street, London, W1N 1DD.

Disabled Against Animal Research and Exploitation, 22 The Severn, Grange Estate, Daventry, Northamptonshire, NN11 4QR. (Supported by the disabled and those with chronic illness, DAARE supports humane, non-animal methods of research and social programmes that benefit disabled people).

THE THIRD WORLD

Traidcraft (see above for address) import a variety of goods and crafts from the Third World, guaranteeing a fair deal for workers. Oxfam have also moved some way towards the 'living without cruelty' ideal by selling not only crafts, tea and coffee from Third World nations and recycled clothes but also some shampoos, talcum powders and bath oils not tested on animals, soaps containing only vegetable oils and organic fertilizers. It must be stressed, however, that not all of their cosmetics are cruelty-free.

Useful addresses
Enough, London House, Queens Road, Freshwater, Isle of Wight, PO40 9EP. (This organization funds vegetarian projects in the Third World and promotes a non-meat diet on ethical, economic and ecological grounds.)

Other useful animal organizations
Compassion In World Farming, 20 Lavant Street, Petersfield, Hampshire GU32 3EW.
Chickens' Lib, PO Box 2, Holmfirth, Huddesfield, HD7 1QT
Hunt Saboteurs' Association, PO Box 19, London, SE 9LR.
League Against Cruel Sports, 83–7 Union Street, London, SE1 1SG.

Campaign Against Angling, PO Box 14, Romsey, Southampton, Hants.
Captive Animals Protection Society, 17 Raphael Road, Hove, East Sussex, BM3 5QP.
Scottish Anti-Vivisection Society, 121 West Regent Street, Glasgow, G2 2SD.
Scottish Society for the Prevention of Vivisection, 10 Queensferry Street, Edinburgh, EH2 4PG.
British Union for the Abolition of Vivisection, 16a Crane Grove, London, N7 8LB.
National Anti-Vivisection Society, 51 Harley Street, London, W1N 1DD.
Zoo Check, Cherry Tree Cottage, Coldharbour, Dorking, Surrey, RH5.
Greenpeace, 36 Graham Street, London, N1 8LL.

A FEW OTHER LINKS

Rainforests

We have already hinted at some of the destructive consequences to the rainforests caused by what has become known as 'hamburgerization'. Alas, the fast-food industry is not alone in putting profits before the future of the planet. The forests are also being felled at an alarming rate for the furniture and building trades.

Friends of the Earth issue a guide to the wood you *can* purchase without supporting the destruction of the rainforests.

Aerosols and other environmental issues

By law all aerosols are tested on animals. They also damage the atmosphere by releasing a gas suspected of thinning the ozone layer which protects us from the sun. The fear is, that as damage increases, the world's delicate balance of climate and life-support systems will be altered, causing blighted food crops and vast increases in skin cancers, leukemias, cataracts and other diseases.

For those who wish to learn more about other important environmental issues (plastics, oils, marine pollution are just three of the many subjects not discussed in this book) and possible green alternatives, *The Friends of the Earth Handbook* (see above) is particularly recommended.

Political prisoners

Some people might be offended by any pointed comparison between the thousands of human beings mistreated, imprisoned, tortured or executed because they happen to hold opinions or religious beliefs in opposition to the rulers of their respective countries and the billions of animals imprisoned and killed in abattoirs and vivisection laboratories. Yet similarities do exist. Both humans and animals are imprisoned against their will and, most importantly, denied their precious freedom. Moreover, viviseciton can be accurately described as the extraction of information from prisoners by force.

Without wishing to take the comparison any further, it does seem to me that the arguments set out in this book for excluding animals from the horrors of slaughter and other exploitation is a logical extension from concern for the rights of humans to be free from political or religious persecution.

Useful address

Amnesty International, British Section, 5 Roberts Place, London, EC1 OEJ.

The arms race

New methods of killing people in warfare, be it nuclear, chemical or improved conventional weapons, are all first tested upon animals. Countries ranging from Iran and Iraq to the USA and USSR use animals in warfare research. Great Britain's centre for such ghastly development is the Porton Down Institute near Salisbury, where, in recent years, species ranging from sheep, pigs, monkeys, dogs and guinea-pigs have been subjected to the poisonous effects of hydrogen cyanide and riot-control gases, been poisoned with fungal poisons used in chemical warfare and been shot through the head with ball bearings to investigate the effects of high-velocity missiles. Almost all of these experiments are designed to refine methods by which human beings can kill each other.

From Porton Down come some of the most moving accounts of animal suffering. The following is from an electrician who accidentally strayed onto the wrong floor after his firm had been contracted to carry out work at Porton Down. It illustrates movingly the main argument of this book: first, that inhumanity to animals and humans cannot be separated; and second, that the undeniable capacity for suffering in other living creatures demands a change in our current attitudes.

At first I thought I was ill. I thought I was seeing things, and then I went a little nearer and looked.

It was a little monkey enclosed in a glass cage—a sort of box. Its eyes seemed to be falling out and it couldn't breathe. It was in dreadful, dreadful distress. I forgot everything and went near and said something to it, and it buried its head in its arms and sobbed like a child.

I never slept that night, and next day managed to go back to the same room, but it was nearly finished by then. It had sunk to a little heap at the bottom of the glass case.

Useful addresses
CND, 22–4 Underwood Street, London, N1 7JG.

Campaign against the Arms Trade, 11 Goodwin Street, London, N4 3HQ.

Notes

Introduction

1 H. Salt *Seventy Years among Savages*. Quotation from *The Extended Circle. A Dictionary of Humane Thought*, ed. J. Wynne Tyson (Centaur Press, 1985).

Chapter 1

1 M. Charleston, Calf love, *The Daily Express*, 2 Dec. 1983.
2 M. Looker, Getting together on Design, *Pig Farming*, April 1984.
3 Dwarf matters challenge the 'pound note' gobblers, *Poultry World*, 17 Nov. 1983.
4 Separate sexes for maximum output and returns, *Poultry World*, 14 June 1984.
5 J. Foster, Acid milk saves starving piglets, *Pig Farming*, Sept. 1984.
6 Pig Chat, *Pig Farming*, Oct. 1984.
7 Survivability Factor, *Pig Farming*, June 1985.
8 J. Hunt, Vets want more care put into calf marketing, *Farmers Weekly*, 22 Feb. 1985.
9 New hope for orphan lambs, *The Times*, Nov. 24, 1981.
10 A. Taylor, Should we cut our teeth clipping?, *Pig Farming*, May 1985.
11 Separate sexes for maximum output and returns, *Poultry World*, 14 June 1984.
12 A. Elson, Careful handling key to downgrading, *Poultry World*, 10 Jan. 1986.
13 Reducing post-stun bruising, *Meat Industry*, Jan. 1984.
14 Poor transport causing pig carcase damage, *Scottish Farmer*, 11 Dec. 1982.
15 L. Gerlis, The cases for slaughtering, *Meat Magazine*, November 1986.
16 J. Shewring, Stunning standards are varied, *Meat Industry*, Nov. 1985.

17 R. Waldmire, I wonna be your ham, *Agenda (US)*, Nov./Dec., 84, p. 18.
18 Thomas Hardy, *Jude the Obscure* (Macmillan Papermacs, London and Basingstoke, 1966), p. 71.
19 Flora Thompson, *Country Calendar* (Oxford University Press, Oxford, 1984), pp. 11–13.
20 It's not what you say but the way that you say it, *Meat Trades Journal*, 22 Nov. 1984.
21 R. Dunbar, Learning the language of primates, *New Scientist*, 13 Dec. 1984.
22 M. Bright, *Animal Language*. (BBC Books, London 1984), p. 234.
23 G. Van Putten, Comfort Behaviour in Pigs and its Significance Regarding their Well-being, European Association for Animal Protection 1977.
24 M. Ridley, Engineering leaner times, *Meat Trades Journal*, 2 July 1987.
25 R. Highfield, Brave new era dawning down on the farm, *The Daily Telegraph*, 24 June 1987.

Chapter 2

1 *Diet and Cardiovascular Disease*, COMA report of the panel on Diet in Relation to Cardiovascular Disease, 28 (1984).
2 G. Cannon and C. Walker, *The Food Scandal* (Century Publishing, 1984), p. 17.
3 A. MacDougall, How the case against animals builds up, *Farmers Weekly*, 9 Nov. 1984.
4 *The Lancet*, i (1983). pp. 5–10.
5 Dietary answer to hypertension, *The Times*, 25 Aug. 1985.
6 E. L. Wynder, *Nature*, 286 (1977), p. 284.
7 *The Lancet*, ii, (1983). p. 233.
8 L. Chaitow, *An End to Cancer?* (Thorsons, 1983), p. 48.
9 T. Stapala, Eat your greens and stop cancer, *New Scientist*, 15 Nov. 1984.
10 W. S. Ross, *Readers Digest Selection*, April 1983.
11 B. R. Golden et al., *New England Journal of Medicine*, 307 (1982), pp. 1542–7.
12 *Journal of National Cancer Institute*, 67 (1981), pp. 761–7.
13 Reported in Information Sheet B1, Environmental Therapy Research, London.
14 D. Burkitt, *Don't Forget Fibre in Your Diet* (Martin Dunitz, 1979).
15 Health Education Council advertisements. See for example, *The Daily Mirror*, 28 Feb. 1983.
16 A. Palgi, *American Journal of Clinical Nutrition*, 37 (1983), pp. 687–8.

17 J. A. Birbeck, *New Zealand Medical Journal*, 94 (1981), pp. 386–9.
18 Vegetarian diet. Fewer diseases, *The Daily Telegraph*, 14 March 1986.
19 F. Pixley, *The Vegetarian*, Nov./Dec. 1984.
20 Diet, Nutrition and Health Report of the Board of Science and Education, B.M.A., 1986.
21 T. A. B. Sanders, Vegetarian diets, *Nutrition Bulletin*, 5 (1979), pp. 137–44.
22 M. L. Burr et al., Plasma cholesterol and blood pressure in vegetarians, *Journal of Human Nutrition*, 35 (1981), pp. 437–44.
23 A. Lockie et al., *Journal of Royal College of General Practitioners*, 35, (1985), pp. 333–6.
24 M. Thorogood and J. Mann, An Epidemological Study of Vegetarians and Vegans, Department of Community Medicine, University of Oxford, Frey Ellis Memorial Lecture, 10 July 1986.
25 Red meat report slammed by M.L.C. *Meat Trades Journal*, 19 June 1986.
26 Chicken tests spark rumpus. *Meat Trades Journal*, 2 October 1986.
27 C. Walker and G. Cannon (1984), *The Food Scandal*, Century Publishing, p. 151.

Chapter 3

1 O. Schell, *Modern Meat* (Random House Books, USA, 1984), p. 6.
2 *Animal Pharm.*, 132, 26 June 1987.
3 Quick cocktails for a lean carcase, *Farmers Weekly*, 14 Sep. 1984, p. 35.
4 D. Burch, What makes pigs cough, *Pig Farming Supplement*, Oct. 1984.
5 Nasty problem, *Pig Farming*, June 1985, p. 7.
6 O. Schell, *Modern Meat*, p. 104.
7 Cited in F. Pearce and J. Cherfas, Antibiotics breed lethal food poisons, *New Scientist*, 13 September 1984.
8 Salmonella—on the rise, *Farmers Weekly*, 25 Jan. 1985, p. 26.
9 Salmonella—on the rise, *Farmers Weekly*, 25 Jan. 1985, p. 26.
10 Salmonellosis: what prospects for future control, *Veterinary Record*, 22 Sept. 1984.
12 Question mark hangs over ban on Promoters, *Meat Trades Journal*, 25 Sept. 1986.
12 R. Collins, Uncowed by hormone count, *The Guardian*, 30 Nov. 1986.
13 O. Schell, *Modern Meat*, p. 187.
14 P. Pallott, Growing fat on the back of drugs, *The Daily Telegraph*, 4 Nov. 1985.

15 M. Cooke, Get tougher over hormones says vet, *Meat Traders Journal*, 21 Nov. 1985.

16 O. Schell, *Modern Meat*, p. 268.

17 Ibid., pp. 272–3.

18 Pill aids gilt management, *Pig Farming*, March 1986.

19 G. Harvey, New hormone will transform Western dairying, *New Scientist*, 2 Oct. 1986.

20 *Meat Trades Journal*, 2 July 1987.

21 Union Warns of health dangers in abattoirs, *Meat Trades Journal*, 13 Sept. 1984.

22 Workers call for probe in cancer fear, *Meat Trades Journal*, 22 May 1986.

23 B. Sheard, *Meat Industry*, April 1985.

24 Blood and bacteria on the abattoir floor, *New Scientist*, 2 Oct. 1986.

25 How to defeat the flying squad, *Meat Trades Journal*, 1 May 1986.

26 O. Smith, Renderers seek last gasp help, *Meat Trades Journal*, 28 August, 1986.

27 How we got our alarming results, *Meat Industry*, Oct. 1983.

28 J. Walsh, *The Meat Machine* (Columbus Books, 1986), p. 84.

29 Colour is important to consumers, *Meat Trades Journal*, 17 April 1986.

30 J. Walsh, *The Meat Machine*, pp. 78–9.

31 Ibid., pp. 82–3. See also 'Sulphur dioxide stops bacteria' and 'M.L.C. expert defends use of nitrates', both *Meat Trades Journal* , 17 April 1986 and 'Here's the Beef', *The Guardian*, 22 Feb. 1985.

Chapter 4

1 V. Wheelock, Cut it by 25%—and that's official, *Farmers Weekly*, 21 Dec. 1984.

2 C. Walker and G. Cannon, *The Food Scandal* (Century Publishing, 1984).

3 What's all the mystery about milk?, *Healthy Living*, July 1984.

4 Cited in A. Robeznieks, The perfect food? Not everyone Agrees, *Vegetarian Times (USA)*, April 1987

5 United Animal Defender Inc. USA, Cleveland, Ohio, Leaflet on factory farming 1983.

6 G. Harvey, Poor cow, *New Scientist*, 29 Sept. 1983.

7 *Meat Trades Journal*, 19 Nov. 1987.

8 A. Robeznieks, The perfect food? Not everyone agrees, *Vegetarian Times (USA)*, April 1987.

Chapter 5

1 N. Twose, *Cultivating Hunger* (Oxfam, Oxford, 1984).
2 Figures from A. Moyes, *Common Ground* (Oxfam, Oxford, 1985).
3 M. Byrn, The future for soy foods, *Food Manufacturers International*, Mar./April 1985.
4 Figures from HM Customs and Excise Statistical Department, 1983.
5 Figures from Oxfam Hungry for Change Campaign.
6 *Dairy Farmer*, Dec. 1984, p. 26.
7 Cereal chief calls for industry marketing body, *Poultry World*, 17 Jan. 1985.
8 Dutch symposium focus on growth rates, *World Poultry*, Aug. 1984.
9 N. Twose, *Cultivating Hunger* (Oxfam, Oxford, 1984).
10 Shortage of feed raw materials, *World Poultry*, April 1985.
11 Ethiopia plans more state farms for layers and broilers, *World Poultry*, April 1985.
12 D. Greenwood, Compounding moves up from concentrates, *World Poultry*, April 1985.
13 Oxfam project 1984.
14 Leaf nutrient literature produced by Find Your Feet, 42 Queen Anne's Gate, London.
15 Feeding the World, *New Scientist*, 30 July 1987.
16 J. Richards, You are what you eat, *The Guardian*, 21 Nov. 1986.
17 C. Aubert (tr. M. Langman), *Nutrition and Health*, 2 (1983).

Chapter 6

1 P. Singer, *In Defense of Animals*, Basil Blackwell, Oxford, 1985.
2 Humane control of pests, *Veterinary Record*, 6 Oct. 1984.
3 K. Jannaway, *Towards A Solution of The World Food Problem* (Vegan Society, 1983).
4 M. Ingram, Outlook for Meat, George Scott Robertson Memorial Lecture, University of Belfast, 1970.
5 The composition and nutritive value of white lupins, *Nutrition Abstracts and Reviews*, Ser. B, 47 (8) (1977).
6 Sunflowers take their time to come to Britain, *Farmers Weekly*, June 1985.
7 Looks like beef . . . tastes like beef . . . comes from a fungus, *Meat Industry*, March 1985.
8 *New Scientist*, 8 Dec. 1977, pp. 626–9.
9 M. Shoard, *The Theft of the Countryside* (Temple-Smith Books, 1980).
10 *Are Your Meals Costing the Earth?* (Vegan Society leaflet, 1986).

11 K. Akers, *Vegetarian Sourcebook* (Vegetarian Press [PO Box 10238, Arlington, Virginia, 22210, USA], 1983).
12 *Dairy Farming*, Dec. 1984.
13 *New Scientist*, 8 Dec. 1977, pp. 626–9.

Chapter 7

1 N. Twose, *Cultivating Hunger* (Oxfam, Oxford, 1984).
2 *Pall of Poison. The Spray Drift Problem* (Soil Association, Bristol, 1984).
3 *New Scientist*, 4 July 1985.
4 R. Carson, *Silent Spring* (Penguin, Harmondsworth, 1962).
5 J. Erlichman, Crop of ailments could be the price of farm spraying, *The Guardian*, 13 March 1985.
6 *Friends of the Earth Handbook* (Optima Books, 1987).
7 Mark Twain, quoted in, *Mark Twain: The Man and His Work*, E. Wagenknecht.
8 *London Evening Standard*, 16 May 1987.
9 E. Millstone, Food additives: a technology out of control, *New Scientist*, 18 Oct. 1984.
10 L. Leigh, Who says it's safe, *The Sunday Times Magazine*, 3 Nov. 1985.
11 C. Moorhead, Killer chemicals—Third World beware, *The Times*, 10 July 1984.

Chapter 8

1 Times Health Supplement, 27 Nov. 1981.
2 *Selection of Essential Drugs*, report of World Health Organisation Expert Committee, 1977, technical report series 615.
3 H. Ridley, *Drugs of Choice—A Report on the Drug Formulas as used in NHS Hospitals* (Social Audit, London, 1986).
4 Medical Research Council annual report, 1982/83.
5 Muddled medical thinking, *Outrage!* (magazine of Animal Aid), 30 (Jan./Feb. 1984).
6 A. Melville and C. Johnston, *Alternatives to Drugs* (Fontana, 1987), p. 18.)
7 *Adverse Drug Reactions Bulletin*, 80 (Feb. 1980).
8 D. Gould, *The Medical Mafia* (Sphere, 1987).
9 P. Ronner, *Too Good to be True, Animal Experiments in Drug Research* (Plasma Information [Ciba-Geigy, Rosche, Sandoz], Basle, Switzerland, 1983).
10 The Rational Health Campaign newsletter, Oxfam, Nov. 1983.
11 S. Braford, Brazil—Where the president is a hypochondriac, *New Internationalist*, Nov. 1986.

12 *Selection of Essential Drugs*, WHO, pp. 9–10.
13 R. Sharpe, The cruel deception, *Animals Defender*, May/June 1985.
14 R. Dubos, *Mirage of Health* (New York, 1959).
15 D. Gould, *The Medical Mafia* (Sphere, 1987).
16 D. Salers and R. Carver, *The Struggle for Health. Medicine and the Politics of Underdevelopment* (Macmillan, London, 1986).
17 *The Lancet*, 15 April 1972.
18 *British Medical Journal*, 27 March 1982.
19 C. T. Dollery, *Risk – Benefit Analysis in Drug Research*, 1981.
20 *New Scientist*, 26 May 1977.
21 R. Ryder, *Victims of Science* (National Anti-Vivisection Society, London), pp. 108–13.
22 R. Sharpe, *The Cruel Deception* (Thorsons, 1988).

Chapter 9

1 Another £7m for M.L.C. meat promotion, *Meat Trades Journal*, 29 Jan. 1987.
2 Sixth report of the Cosmetics Review expert panel, *Journal of American College of Toxicology*, 13 (1984).
3 C. Hepper, *Herbal Cosmetics*, (Thorsons, 1987).
4 E. V. Buchler and E. A. Newmann, *Toxicology and Applied Pharmacology*, 6 (1964), pp. 701–10.
5 *New Scientist*, 23 June 1977.
6 *Journal of National Cancer Institute*, 67.
7 P. J. Lewis, *Archives of Technology*, suppl. 5 (1982), pp. 195–6.
8 Report in *The Guardian* cited in *Outrage!*, 42 (Jan./Feb. 1986), p. 8.
9 *British National Formula*, II, (1986) (BMA and Pharmaceutical Society of Great Britain), p. 127.
10 D. Musselwhite, The fur fighter, *Green Cuisine*, Sept./Oct. 1986.
11 This bloody disgrace is called museling. *Animal Liberation (Australia)*, 1986.
12 J. de Bairacli Levy, *Complete Herbal Handbook for Dogs and Cats* (Faber & Faber).
13 *The Medway (Cranbrook) Report. An Enquiry Into Shooting and Angling*, (RSPCA, 1980).

Chapter 10

1 T. A. B. Sanders, Vegetarian diets, *Nutrition Bulletin*, 5 (1979), pp. 137–244.
2 T. A. B. Sanders and R. Purves, An anthropomorphic and dietary assessment of the nutritional status of vegan pre-school children, *Journal of Human Nutrition*, 1981, pp. 35, 349, 357.

3 R. Elliot, The Vegetarian Mother and Baby Book (Fontana, 1984).
4 Soya beats cow's milk in infant diarrhoea, *Journal of Alternative Medicine*, July 1986.
5 D. Fletcher, Row over teenage diet report, *The Daily Telegraph*, 3 April 1986.
6 H. Wright, Swallow it whole, *New Statesman* report 4, p. 9.
7 p. 13.
8 The way to a pupil's stomach is through his heart, *The Guardian*, 23 Sept. 1986.
9 K. Akers, *The Vegetarian Sourcebook* (Vegetarian Press, PO Box 10238, Arlington, Virginia, 22210, USA).
10 H. Kirby, One child's meat, *The Times*, 25 Feb. 1988.

Part 2: Recipes

1 T. A. B. Sanders, Dietetic and medical aspects, *Journal of Plant Foods*, 1983.